Rebirth Behind Bars

Healing and Personal Growth, Volume 3

Arturo José Sánchez Hernández

Published by Arturo José Sánchez Hernández, 2024.

REBIRTH BEHIND BARS

First edition. November 14, 2024.

ISBN: 979-8230714576

Written by Arturo José Sánchez Hernández.

Table of Contents

PREFACE

This book you hold in your hands is not just a collection of words, but an invitation to a journey of inner transformation. *Rebirth Behind Bars* is born out of the need to give a voice to those who, behind the walls of a prison, have found hope, resilience, and the power to build a new version of themselves. Though the bars may be physical, often the most challenging barriers to overcome are those we have built within ourselves.

For those who find themselves deprived of freedom, the challenge is not just to serve a sentence but also to face their own mistakes, acknowledge them, and use them as a springboard towards a better life. *Rebirth Behind Bars* is a path to freedom that begins within the soul, from the deep desire for change and the will to transform suffering into personal growth.

This book aims to be a beacon of hope, a companion on the journey that shows pain can be harnessed, that a fall does not define the future, and that each person has the power to decide what kind of story they want to write. Through lessons of resilience, practical strategies, and personal reflections, *Rebirth Behind Bars* seeks to help transform darkness into light, to build a more dignified and free future, regardless of the present circumstances.

It is not about erasing the past but learning from it, finding inner peace through forgiveness, gratitude, and reconciliation. This book is written for all those who, regardless of their situation, seek a new opportunity to be reborn, to free themselves from the weight of their mistakes, and to build a better version of themselves.

I hope these pages inspire you to see beyond the visible and invisible bars and help you find the power and light that reside within you. This journey is difficult, but the reward —inner freedom— is immensely valuable.

With respect and hope,

Dr. Arturo José Sánchez Hernández.

The Author.

~~~

THE POWER OF HOPE: TRANSFORMING DARKNESS INTO LIGHT

Hope is one of the most powerful forces we can cultivate, especially during moments of great adversity. In life, we all face difficult situations, and being in prison can feel like the end of everything we know and love. However, hope has the power to transform us, to be that small but steady spark that lights the way when everything seems shrouded in darkness.

The Seed of Hope

Imagine a seed in the middle of dry, cracked soil. That seed, seemingly alone, is surrounded by unfavorable conditions. Yet, despite it all, it holds within itself the strength to sprout and grow. Hope acts the same way in our lives: it is the force that keeps us steady and pushes us to grow, even when everything seems against us.

Hope in Prison

Being in prison can be a time of immense darkness and uncertainty. The days may feel endless, and the routine can wear down your spirit. But it is in these very moments that hope becomes essential. Having hope means believing that, even though today is hard, tomorrow can be better. It means trusting that your time in prison can become an opportunity for personal growth, self-discovery, and reflection. It can be a time to rediscover yourself and decide what kind of person you want to be.

The Reality and Power of Hope

Hope does not mean ignoring reality or sugarcoating what is happening. It allows us to recognize challenges and difficulties while giving us purpose—a reason to rise each morning, even in the hardest times. It is the tool that enables us to see beyond the walls that surround us, envision a better future, and, most importantly, work to make it a reality.

Small Actions That Nurture Hope

Hope is nourished by small actions. Every step you take to improve, every effort to learn something new, every day you choose to keep going is an act of hope. Over time, those small actions create big changes. It could be learning a new skill, helping someone, writing down your thoughts, or exercising to take care of your body. Even moments of self-reflection or offering a kind word to another person can be powerful. Each of these things, no matter how small they seem, contributes to the transformation you seek within yourself and builds momentum toward a brighter future.

Examples of Transformation Through Hope

History is full of examples of people who, despite facing extreme situations—even the harsh realities of prison—found the strength to move forward, reinvent themselves, and make significant contributions to society. These stories were not forged in ease or comfort, but in perseverance and steadfast hope: a vision of a brighter future that gave them the courage to endure and grow. Hope powerfully reminds us that we are not defined by our circumstances, but by our ability to overcome them, inspiring us to continually seek growth and transformation.

FINAL CONSIDERATIONS

If you find yourself in a dark place today, remember that darkness is not forever. Hope is the light that can guide you, and even if it's small, it's enough to take the next step. Keep that hope alive. Believe in the future you want to build, and use each day to take one more step toward it.

~~~

KEEP HOPE ALIVE: PRACTICAL STRATEGIES TO KEEP MOVING FORWARD

In life, hope is that spark that drives us to keep going, even when everything feels difficult. For those in prison, where the environment can often feel discouraging, finding ways to keep hope alive is essential. Hope is not just a feeling; it is a choice and a habit that is cultivated day by day. Today, let's explore some practical strategies to help you keep that flame alive and move forward, one step at a time.

Visualize a Better Future

One of the most powerful ways to keep hope alive is to visualize a better future. Imagination has immense power—it allows you to project yourself into a different place from where you are now and build a bridge between your present and that desired future. Picture what you'd like your life to look like after your release: reuniting with loved ones, finding a job you're passionate about, or simply living a peaceful life. Let your mind wander through these possibilities, allowing yourself to dream freely. Spend a few minutes each day on this visualization, detailing each image and feeling the emotions of those future moments. Keeping that vision in your mind will remind you why it's worth moving forward.

Focus on Small Daily Achievements

Being in prison can make the days feel monotonous, but finding small daily accomplishments can shift your perspective and fuel your hope. Did you learn something new today? Have a meaningful conversation? Exercise, write a paragraph, or experience a moment of calm? These are all achievements. You don't need major successes to celebrate. Small steps matter, and each one is proof that you're moving toward a better future. Making a list of your daily achievements, no matter how small, can be a powerful tool for maintaining a positive mindset.

Surround Yourself with Positive Thoughts

Our thoughts have a direct impact on how we feel and face each day. It's easy to get caught up in negative thinking, especially in a challenging environment like prison. However, surrounding yourself with positive thoughts can make a big difference. Start each day with a positive affirmation, such as "Today I can do something to improve my life" or "I have the ability to change my future." Write encouraging phrases and place them where you can see them, or repeat them to yourself when you're feeling down. Also, try to surround yourself with people who, despite being in the same circumstances, strive to maintain a constructive attitude. Sharing words of encouragement and mutual support can help keep hope alive for everyone.

Practice Gratitude

Gratitude is essential for cultivating hope. Despite the challenges, there is always something to be grateful for: a letter received, an honest conversation, the simple fact of waking up another day with the chance to improve. Practicing gratitude helps you focus on what you have instead of what you lack, and that becomes a constant source of hope. Each day, find at least one thing you're grateful for and reflect on it.

Take Care of Your Body and Mind

Keeping hope alive also depends on taking care of your physical and mental well-being. Regular exercise, even in a small space, helps release tension and maintain a positive mood. Practicing meditation or mindful breathing can calm your mind and connect you to the present moment. When you take care of your body and mind, you're sending yourself a message: "I matter, and I'm working on myself."

FINAL CONSIDERATIONS

Keeping hope alive in a place where time feels like it has stopped is not easy, but it is possible. Visualizing a better future, celebrating small achievements, surrounding yourself with positive thoughts, practicing gratitude, and taking care of your physical and mental well-being are tools that will help you sustain that hope. Day by day, remember that darkness doesn't last forever, and the light you need is within you, waiting to be ignited.

~~~

THE IMPORTANCE OF A POSITIVE MINDSET: CHANGING FROM WITHIN

The way we think deeply affects how we live. This is even more true when we face difficult situations, such as being in prison. In those moments, a positive mindset is not just an optional tool—it's a necessity that can change our perspective on the present and shape our future. It allows us to find meaning in adversity, discover opportunities for growth, and maintain hope even in the darkest times. Cultivating a positive attitude has the power to transform our reality, influence our decisions, and, most importantly, improve our emotions. Here, we will explore why a positive mindset is essential and how to begin creating that change from within.

Internal Change Starts with Attitude

A positive attitude doesn't mean ignoring problems or pretending everything is fine when it's not. It's about adopting a perspective that allows us to see challenges as opportunities to learn and grow. A positive attitude is the first step toward internal change because it alters how we interpret what happens to us. Instead of feeling stuck or powerless, we begin to see possibilities, even in the face of adversity.

External circumstances aren't always under our control, but our attitude is. When we choose to be positive, we decide to focus on what we can do instead of what we can't. That choice impacts our emotions, giving us the strength and resilience to face each day.

How a Positive Mindset Influences Decisions

A positive mindset not only improves our emotional state but also influences the quality of our decisions. When faced with a challenge, a negative attitude can lead to despair or discouragement, causing us to make impulsive decisions or give up. In contrast, a positive mindset allows us to calmly analyze situations, explore our options, and choose the best course of action.

For instance, by focusing on what you can do, you'll start making decisions that benefit you. You might choose to learn a new skill, read an inspiring book, or work on improving a relationship. These small steps, guided by a positive mindset, become meaningful decisions that move you closer to a better future. As you consistently make these choices, you begin to build momentum that propels you forward, strengthening your sense of purpose and direction.

Impact on Emotions

Our thoughts and emotions are closely connected. A negative mindset feeds emotions like anger, frustration, or sadness. On the other hand, choosing positive thoughts nurtures healthier emotions like hope, peace, and joy. This doesn't mean you'll never feel sadness or anger, but a positive mindset will help you manage those difficult moments and avoid getting stuck in them.

Thinking positively sends a message to your mind that it's worth pushing forward, that you are capable of overcoming difficulties. This self-confidence strengthens your emotional well-being and allows you to face each day with better energy and determination. Positive thinking also helps you see challenges as opportunities for growth, shifting your focus from obstacles to solutions and possibilities.

Strategies for Cultivating a Positive Mindset

Cultivating a positive mindset is a daily process. It requires consistent effort and the willingness to shift your perspective in the face of challenges. Here are some strategies to help you:

> – **Daily Affirmations**: Start each morning with positive affirmations like "Today, I will give my best" or "I have the power to change my life." These simple phrases have a powerful impact when repeated with conviction.
>
> – **Focus on the Positive**: Even on hard days, try to find something positive. It could be a small achievement, a kind conversation, or simply the fact that you've stayed strong so far.
>
> – **Surround Yourself with Good Influences**: The thoughts of those around you also affect your mindset. Seek out people who want to improve, who are positive, and who support each other.

– **Practice Gratitude**: Take a moment each day to reflect on what you're grateful for. This helps you focus on the good in your life and feel more optimistic.

FINAL CONSIDERATIONS

A positive mindset is the key to initiating internal change and transforming your reality. While you can't change all your circumstances, you can change how you face them. With a positive attitude, you can influence your decisions, improve your emotions, and ultimately build a more fulfilling life—even in the darkest moments. Remember, while you may not control everything that happens to you, you can control how you respond to it.

~~~

THE POWER OF RESILIENCE: RISE AND GROW WITH EVERY FALL

Life is full of challenges, difficult moments, and falls that sometimes feel impossible to overcome. Yet, there is a quality that allows us not only to survive these hardships but to emerge from them stronger and wiser: resilience. Resilience is the ability to rise after every fall, to transform pain and adversity into opportunities for growth. Today, I want to talk to you about the power of resilience and how it can help you transform your life, even in the most challenging circumstances.

What Is Resilience?

Resilience is that inner strength that drives you to keep moving forward, even when everything seems to be against you. It is the ability to adapt, learn, and grow from difficult experiences. Resilience doesn't mean we don't feel pain or that challenges don't affect us; it means that despite the pain, we choose to get back up and keep fighting for a better future.

When you are in prison, it can be easy to feel like the world has stopped and the future is uncertain. But it's precisely in these moments of adversity that resilience becomes most important. Being resilient doesn't just mean surviving your time in prison—it means coming out of this experience stronger, wiser, and ready to build a better life.

Learn from Every Fall

In life, we all experience falls. Sometimes we make mistakes, take the wrong path, or face the consequences of our actions. But these falls don't have to define us. Every fall is an opportunity to learn, to reflect on what led us to that point, and to find ways to do better in the future.

Resilience allows you to look at every mistake, every obstacle, and ask yourself, "What can I learn from this?" Instead of seeing difficulties as the end of the road, you can view them as part of the growth process. Every fall is a lesson, and every time you rise, you are closer to becoming the person you want to be. Resilience teaches you not to give up, to hold onto hope, and to use every experience as a stepping stone toward a better future.

Resilience as Strength for the Future

Being resilient doesn't just mean surviving difficult moments; it means coming out of them with a new perspective and the strength to face what lies ahead. Resilience helps you see beyond current challenges and focus on future possibilities. When you are resilient, you realize that no matter how difficult the past has been, you can always rise and build something new.

Every day is a new opportunity to be resilient. It could be something as simple as maintaining a positive attitude, learning something new, or committing to improving an area of your life. These small acts of resilience add up and prepare you for greater challenges. Resilience isn't about being invincible; it's about being flexible, adapting, and learning. It's the strength that allows you to transform difficulties into opportunities for growth.

How to Cultivate Resilience

Accept Difficulties: Life has tough moments, and accepting them is the first step toward resilience. Don't fight reality; focus on how to overcome challenges.

Find the Lesson in Every Situation: Every experience, no matter how hard, has something to teach us. Always look for the lesson and use it to grow and improve.

Maintain a Positive Mindset: Your attitude toward challenges makes all the difference. Stay hopeful and focus on possibilities instead of limitations.

Take Care of Your Well-Being: Resilience also means taking care of yourself. Exercise, eat well, get enough sleep, and spend time on activities that make you feel good. A strong body supports a strong mind.

Surround Yourself with Positive Support: The people around you can be a great source of encouragement. Seek relationships that inspire you, uplift you, and help you stay motivated during tough times.

FINAL CONSIDERATIONS

Resilience is the ability to rise after every fall, to transform pain and adversity into opportunities for growth. Being resilient doesn't mean you won't feel the pain of challenges—it means that despite it, you choose to keep going and fight for a better future. Every fall is a lesson, and every time you rise, you become stronger and better prepared to face what's ahead. Today, I encourage you to develop resilience, to remember that you can always rise, and to see every difficulty as just one part of the journey toward a stronger, wiser life.

~~~

USE YOUR PAIN: BUILD A BETTER VERSION OF YOURSELF

Pain is an experience that everyone faces at some point in life. It can be physical, emotional, or spiritual, and it often feels like a burden that holds us back. However, suffering also has the potential to be a powerful tool for personal growth. For those in prison, pain may feel overwhelming, but it can also become the driving force behind positive transformation. Today, let's reflect on how suffering and difficult experiences can be a means to build a better version of ourselves.

Pain as an Opportunity for Growth

When we go through painful moments, it's natural to want to escape, avoid, or stop feeling altogether. Yet pain also has a transformative side. In those moments of greatest vulnerability, we come face to face with our weaknesses, fears, and insecurities. It is precisely in this vulnerability that the opportunity for growth lies.

Pain forces us to reflect on who we are and what we want for our future. Instead of seeing it as an enemy, we can view it as a teacher that pushes us to change, improve, and develop skills we might not have discovered otherwise. Accepting suffering as part of the growth process gives us the strength to transform ourselves and find purpose even in the most difficult situations.

Strengthen Yourself Internally

Difficult experiences have the potential to strengthen us from within. It's not about ignoring the pain but facing it with courage. Each time you choose to confront pain instead of running from it, you develop resilience and cultivate an inner strength that enables you to overcome any obstacle.

Think of pain as the process of forging steel. For steel to become stronger, it must go through fire. Similarly, painful experiences are the fire that, while burning, also allows us to grow stronger. When you learn to endure pain and use it as a source of motivation, you are forging a more resilient version of yourself.

Transform Yourself Through Suffering

Many people have found in suffering the spark they needed to change their lives. Pain can be the turning point that drives you to make different decisions, commit to a better future, and break away from past patterns that no longer serve you. Reflecting on mistakes, learning from them, and using those lessons to transform yourself is one of the most powerful ways to use pain for good.

Being in prison can be an experience filled with pain, loneliness, and regret. But it can also be a time to reflect and rediscover who you are and who you want to be. Instead of letting pain consume you, use it to fuel your desire to improve, find purpose, and build a meaningful life. Every moment of suffering is an opportunity to grow, understand yourself better, and commit to positive change.

Strategies to Use Pain as a Tool for Growth

– **Write Your Emotions**: Putting your feelings into words is an effective way to process pain. Keeping a journal helps you better understand your emotions and see how those experiences contribute to your growth.

– **Reflect on Lessons Learned**: Every painful experience carries a lesson. Reflect on what you've learned and how those lessons can help you become a better version of yourself.

– **Seek Support**: Talking to others about your pain, sharing your experiences, and listening to theirs can help you feel less alone and find new perspectives. Mutual support is a powerful tool for transformation.

– **Set Goals Inspired by Pain**: Use your pain as motivation to set goals. Start small, like improving an aspect of your health or learning something new. Each goal you achieve reminds you that pain doesn't define you—you are the one in control.

FINAL CONSIDERATIONS

Pain is an inevitable part of life, but it can also be a powerful tool for personal growth. By facing suffering with courage, you can transform it into a driving force to build a better version of yourself. While difficult experiences may feel insurmountable, every moment of pain is an opportunity to reflect, grow, and strengthen yourself internally. Remember, though pain may be part of your story, it doesn't have to be the end. You have the power to use that suffering to create a new beginning—one that is stronger and filled with purpose.

~~~

TURN YOUR MISTAKES INTO LESSONS: YOUR FUTURE IS NOT DEFINED BY YOUR PAST

We all make mistakes. It's part of being human. The mistakes of the past can be painful, bring regret, and make us feel as though there's no way to make amends. However, what matters most isn't the mistake itself, but what.we do after we've made it. Mistakes don't have to define your future. They can become powerful lessons that help you grow and improve. Here, you are invited to see your past mistakes not as chains tying you to guilt, but as opportunities for learning and growth.

Mistakes Don't Define Who You Are

Sometimes, it's easy to think that because we've made mistakes, we no longer have the ability to change. You might feel the weight of your past decisions and believe that's all you'll ever be. But that's a misconception. Your past doesn't have to define who you are or who you'll become. Every mistake can be an opportunity to reflect, learn, and improve.

The first step to turning a mistake into a lesson is accepting that everyone, without exception, makes mistakes. What matters is what we do with those experiences. Will you remain stuck in guilt, or will you choose to learn and grow from it? The choice is yours, and the good news is that you can always choose to move forward.

Mistakes as Opportunities for Learning

When you make a mistake, you have two options: dwell on it endlessly and stay trapped in the past, or learn from the experience and use it to build a better future. Mistakes teach us valuable lessons about ourselves and the world around us. They reveal our weaknesses and areas for improvement and motivate us to become more mindful of our decisions in the future.

Every mistake holds a lesson, and it's up to you to find it. If you made a poor choice, ask yourself: "What led me to make that decision?" "What could I do differently next time?" By analyzing mistakes objectively and without self-judgment, you give yourself the opportunity to learn and become a better version of yourself. Remember that every experience, even negative ones, can be a source of growth if you choose to see it that way.

Free Yourself from the Chains of Guilt

Guilt is a heavy burden that holds you back. Feeling guilty after making a mistake is natural, but staying trapped in guilt won't help you grow or change. Guilt keeps you tied to the past, while learning propels you toward the future. To turn your mistakes into lessons, it's important to let go of guilt and focus on what you can do today to improve.

Remember, letting go of guilt doesn't mean ignoring your mistakes; it means acknowledging them, taking responsibility, and using them as stepping stones to build a better future.

Forgiveness, especially self-forgiveness, is a crucial step in this process. Forgiving yourself doesn't mean excusing your mistakes—it means acknowledging that you are human, that you made an error, and that you're willing to learn from it. By freeing yourself from guilt, you create space for growth and the possibility of writing a new chapter in your life.

How to Turn Mistakes into Lessons

- **Reflect on the Mistake**: Take time to think about what happened. Analyze what led you to make that mistake and what you could have done differently. Reflection is key to learning and avoiding repeating the same mistakes in the future.

- **Identify the Lesson**: Ask yourself what you can learn from the experience. Maybe you learned something about yourself, your limits, or the importance of listening to others. Identifying the lesson helps you turn the mistake into something positive.

- **Commit to Change**: Once you've identified the lesson, commit to change. Define how you'll act differently the next time you face a similar situation. Commitment to change is what allows you to grow and evolve.

- **Forgive Yourself**: Let go of guilt and understand that making mistakes is part of being human. Forgive yourself and focus on the present—on what you can do today to be better.

FINAL CONSIDERATIONS

The mistakes of the past don't have to define your future. Every mistake can be an opportunity for learning and growth if you choose to see it that way. Instead of staying stuck in guilt, choose to turn your mistakes into lessons that help you become a better version of yourself. Remember that the past is behind you, but the future is full of possibilities. You have the power to change and to build a better future, using every lesson learned to move forward with strength and wisdom.

~~~

YOU DECIDE WHAT STORY TO WRITE: BUILDING YOUR OWN FUTURE

In life, we all have a story, and each day is a new blank page that offers us the opportunity to write the next chapter. Sometimes, the past can feel like a weight holding us back, filled with mistakes, dark moments, and regrets. But what truly matters is not how the story began, but how we decide it will continue. Every new day gives you the chance to turn the page and start anew, no matter how heavy the past may seem. Remember that you are the author of your life, and you have the power to decide what kind of story you want to write from now on. With wiser and more intentional decisions, you can create a future full of hope, growth, and possibilities.

The Past Does Not Define Your Future

The past is part of your story, but it doesn't have to define your future. Even if you've faced hardships or made mistakes, you always have the ability to change the course of your life. Each day is a new opportunity to write a new chapter, one in which you choose to be stronger, wiser, and more mindful of your decisions.

It's easy to feel that, because of past mistakes, we don't deserve a better future or that our options are limited. But that isn't true. Each of us has the power to change our story. The choices you make today will determine the kind of life you'll have tomorrow. By taking control of your personal narrative, you can leave your mistakes behind and choose the path you truly want to follow.

Take Control of Your Personal Narrative

Taking control of your narrative means deciding how you want your story to unfold, even if the beginning wasn't perfect. Imagine your life as a book, and you are the author. The previous chapters are already written, but the next one is still blank. You get to decide how to write it, what changes to make, and what new opportunities to create.

Start by reflecting on the kind of person you want to be. How do you want to be remembered? What values will guide your decisions? These questions are fundamental to taking control of your narrative and defining the path you want to follow. By doing this, you realize that the power to change and create a new story lies within you.

No matter how dark the past has been, you can always choose a new path. Every day, you can make decisions that bring you closer to the person you want to be. Each small effort counts: learning something new, being kind to yourself, helping others, or developing a positive habit. All of this contributes to the story you're writing. You decide whether the next chapter will be one of growth, resilience, and hope.

Make Conscious Choices for a Better Future

To write a better story, it's important to make intentional choices. Many of the mistakes we've made in the past happened because we acted without thinking, without considering the consequences. Now is the time to change that. Every decision has the power to bring you closer to or further from the future you want. By being mindful of your choices, reflecting before you act, and choosing wisely, you take control of your life and create a different story.

Deciding what kind of story to write also means surrounding yourself with people who support, inspire, and encourage you to be better. Build relationships that push you to grow, remind you of your ability to change, and give you the strength to move forward. By surrounding yourself with positive influences and making decisions that reflect your values, you'll be writing a chapter filled with hope and possibility.

Every decision matters, even the smallest ones. Significant changes often start with simple steps. A single good decision, made at the right time, can be the catalyst for transforming your entire story.

FINAL CONSIDERATIONS

You decide what story to write. Even if the past holds dark moments, that doesn't mean the future has to be the same. Each day is a new opportunity to take control of your personal narrative and decide how you want your life to unfold. With wiser and more intentional decisions, you can build a future full of hope, growth, and opportunity. Always remember that the power to change and to write a new story is in your hands. Each day is a blank page, and you are the author.

~~~

BUILD A SOLID FOUNDATION FOR YOUR FUTURE FREEDOM: REACH YOUR TRUE POTENTIAL

Freedom is something we all long for, but true freedom goes beyond simply leaving a physical place. Real freedom means living fully, in peace, with the ability to make wise decisions and build a positive future. Time in prison, though it may feel like life is on pause, is an opportunity to prepare and lay a solid foundation for the future. Today, let's talk about how inner work and personal preparation can be the keys to a successful and fulfilling life once you regain your freedom.

Inner Work: Building Resilience and Peace

Inner work is one of the most powerful ways to prepare for future freedom. It's about getting to know yourself—understanding your emotions, weaknesses, and strengths—and working to become a better version of yourself. Reflect on past experiences and mistakes, but do so without judging yourself. Every mistake is an opportunity to learn, and every day is a new chance to grow.

Practicing meditation, deep breathing, journaling your thoughts and emotions, and dedicating time to personal reflection are effective ways to nurture your inner well-being. The more you understand yourself and find peace within, the better prepared you'll be to face future challenges. The resilience you build now will be your greatest ally when you regain your freedom.

Education and Skills: Preparing for a New Life

Time in prison is also an opportunity to educate yourself and develop skills that will be useful in the future. Education is a powerful tool that can open doors and provide opportunities when you're released. You can learn a trade, improve your formal education, or gain knowledge about topics that interest you. Everything you learn now will help you build a better foundation for a successful and opportunity-filled life.

In addition to formal education, it's important to work on practical skills that will be useful in the outside world. This includes learning how to manage your finances, developing effective communication skills, and improving your problem-solving abilities. These skills will not only help you find job opportunities but also allow you to face life with greater confidence and security.

Strengthen Positive Relationships

Personal relationships are essential for a fulfilling and free life. Use this time to strengthen your connections with those who support you, believe in you, and want to see you succeed. Honest communication and respect are the foundations of any healthy relationship. Rebuilding trust with your loved ones may take time, but every effort counts and can be a great source of support when you regain your freedom.

It's also important to surround yourself with people who encourage you to be better, motivate you to grow, and inspire you to move forward. Stay connected with those who represent a positive influence in your life and learn to identify and distance yourself from negative influences that could steer you away from your goals. Healthy relationships will be key to living a successful and balanced life after prison.

The Value of Purpose

Finding a purpose is one of the most powerful ways to build a solid foundation for the future. Ask yourself what motivates you, what energizes you, and what kind of contribution you want to make to the world. Having a clear purpose will give you direction—something to work toward every day, something that drives you to keep going even during tough times.

Having a purpose will also help you stay focused and avoid falling into old negative patterns. When you have a clear goal and a purpose you're passionate about, you'll feel more motivated to make decisions that bring you closer to that goal and avoid those that might jeopardize your well-being and freedom. This purpose becomes the compass that guides you toward a better and more fulfilling life.

FINAL CONSIDERATIONS

Freedom is much more than leaving a physical place—it's the ability to live a full life, in peace, and with purpose. Use your time in prison to build a solid foundation for your future freedom. Work on your inner well-being, educate yourself, develop practical skills, strengthen positive relationships, and find a purpose that inspires you. Everything you do today will help you be better prepared for the moment you regain your freedom and enable you to build a successful life filled with opportunities, free from the limitations of the past.

~~~

SELF-DISCIPLINE AND A POSITIVE DAILY ROUTINE: BUILDING HEALTHY HABITS FOR A MEANINGFUL LIFE

Self-discipline is the ability to stay focused and determined to achieve your goals, even when circumstances are challenging. In an environment like prison, practicing self-discipline and creating a positive daily routine can be the key to maintaining hope, finding purpose, and strengthening both mind and body. Healthy habits, such as daily exercise, meditation, and activities that bring structure to your day, help you face challenges and foster inner growth. Today, let's discuss the importance of self-discipline and how building a positive daily routine can transform your life, even in difficult circumstances.

Self-Discipline as the Foundation for Transformation

Self-discipline is the ability to take control of your actions and decisions, and it's essential for making positive changes in life. Sometimes it may feel easier to give in to inertia and lose motivation, especially when conditions are less than ideal. However, it's precisely in these moments that self-discipline becomes your greatest ally.

By developing self-discipline, you give yourself the opportunity to create a daily structure that allows you to make the most of your time, keep your mind active, and focus on what truly matters. Self-discipline helps you establish healthy habits that bring meaning to each day, enable gradual improvement, and give you a sense of purpose amidst adversity. Remember, every small effort you make today, no matter how minor it may seem, brings you closer to the best version of yourself.

Create a Positive Routine

A positive daily routine provides structure and stability, which are fundamental for mental and emotional well-being, especially in an environment like prison. Having a set routine helps you stay focused, feel in control of your life, and give each day a sense of purpose. Here are some healthy habits that can be part of a positive daily routine:

– **Daily Exercise**: Exercise is one of the best ways to care for your body and mind. You don't need a gym to work out; you can do simple routines like push-ups, squats, or walking within the available space. Exercise not only improves your physical health but also helps release tension, reduce stress, and boost your mood.

– **Meditation or Mindful Breathing**: Meditation and mindful breathing exercises are excellent ways to calm your mind and reduce anxiety. Spending a few minutes each day meditating or focusing on your breath can help you find inner peace, stay calm, and face challenges with a more positive attitude.

– **Reading and Learning**: Keep your mind active by learning something new every day. Reading is a great way to gain knowledge, expand your perspective, and keep your brain engaged. You can read about topics that interest you, personal development, or anything that inspires you. Learning something new each day helps you grow and maintain motivation.

– **Set Daily Goals**: Setting small goals for each day helps you stay focused and gives you a sense of accomplishment. These goals don't have to be big; they can be as simple as dedicating time to reading, completing an exercise routine, or reflecting on something important. Each goal you achieve strengthens your self-discipline and brings you closer to your larger objectives.

– **Keep a Journal**: Journaling is an excellent way to reflect on your thoughts and emotions. It helps you better understand yourself, process your experiences, and stay connected with your inner self. Spend a few minutes each day writing about your reflections, goals, and achievements—it's a powerful way to give meaning to each day.

The Importance of Consistency

The true power of self-discipline and a positive daily routine lies in consistency. It's not about doing something big once but about making small efforts every day. Consistency allows you to turn those small habits into a lifestyle that strengthens you physically, mentally, and emotionally. Maintaining a daily routine isn't always easy, especially in tough circumstances, but it's precisely in those moments that you need the structure to keep you steady and focused.

Each day is a new opportunity to improve, grow, and take one more step toward the future you want. By maintaining a positive routine and being consistent in your efforts, you're building a solid foundation to face any challenge and make the most of each day, even in a challenging environment.

FINAL CONSIDERATIONS

Self-discipline and a positive daily routine are essential for maintaining physical, mental, and emotional well-being, especially in a difficult setting like prison. Creating healthy habits—such as exercise, meditation, reading, and daily reflection—gives structure and meaning to each day, helps you stay focused, and prepares you to face challenges with a stronger and more positive mindset. Always remember that every small effort counts, and consistency is the key to building a purposeful and meaningful life.

~~~

SMALL STEPS TOWARD CHANGE: IMPROVING LITTLE BY LITTLE

When you find yourself in a challenging environment like prison, the idea of change may seem impossible. The limitations of the surroundings, the barriers, and the daily routine can make change feel out of reach. However, any significant transformation begins with a small step. You don't need to overhaul your life overnight; small, consistent steps can help you build something different and positive. Today, let's talk about how, despite difficulties, it's possible to take steps toward change and begin improving your life right now.

The Importance of Small Steps

It's easy to think that only big changes matter, but the truth is that the most lasting changes start small. Every little action—every effort to learn something new or reflect on your mistakes—is a step forward. In prison, it may seem like there are limited options for change, but small steps are a powerful way to keep hope alive and lay the groundwork for a better future.

What's most important is to remember that, even in a challenging environment, your attitude and the decisions you make each day are within your control. These small steps not only help you improve gradually but also prove that you can take charge of your life, even in the toughest circumstances. The key is not to get discouraged; every day matters, and every small effort you make is a seed planted for the future.

Educate Yourself and Learn

One of the most important steps toward change is education. It doesn't have to be a formal program; every book you read and every new thing you learn is a step toward a better you. Education allows you to expand your perspective, understand more about the world, and prepare for the opportunities that will come when you leave prison.

It could be learning a practical skill, such as a trade, or simply reading about topics that interest you. Everything you learn strengthens you and makes you more capable. Additionally, education helps you find a sense of purpose and provides something positive to focus on, keeping your mind active and oriented toward personal growth.

Reflect on Past Mistakes

Another small step toward change is reflection. Taking the time to think about the past and the decisions that brought you here isn't about punishing yourself—it's about learning. Reflecting on mistakes allows you to see how you could act differently in the future and become a better version of yourself.

This process of reflection is key to personal growth and ensuring that when the time comes to leave, you'll be ready to make decisions that lead to a more positive future. Reflection also helps you identify patterns of behavior that have held you back and work on changing them, avoiding the repetition of past mistakes.

Make Plans for the Future

Your environment may be limited, but your mind is infinite. Use this time to make plans for the future. Imagine how you want your life to be when you're out—reconnecting with your family, learning a trade, or working to help others who've been in similar situations.

Making plans gives you a sense of purpose and something to work toward each day. These plans can be as simple as improving your physical health or as ambitious as learning a new profession. The key is to have something that drives you forward and inspires you to be better. Planning also gives you a clear vision of where you want to go, which is crucial for staying motivated during difficult times.

Celebrate Small Wins

Every small step matters, and it's important to recognize and celebrate those achievements. Maybe today you managed to read a chapter of a book, had a meaningful conversation with someone, or simply stayed positive during a tough moment.

These small victories add up and, day by day, make a difference. Celebrating each accomplishment, no matter how small, keeps you motivated and focused on your path to change. It's also a way to acknowledge the effort you're putting in, which helps maintain a positive attitude and the determination to keep going. Every win, no matter how minor, is proof that you're moving forward and that change is possible.

FINAL CONSIDERATIONS

Real change happens gradually, step by step. Each day is a new opportunity to move toward a better future through education, reflection, planning, and celebrating small wins. Even if the journey is tough, every effort, no matter how small, brings you closer to the person you want to be and builds a future full of opportunities.

~~~

MAKE CONSTRUCTIVE USE OF YOUR TIME IN PRISON: TIME IS LIFE

Time is one of the most valuable resources we have. Regardless of the circumstances, every moment counts and can be used to move forward. For those in prison, it's easy to feel like time is standing still, that the days are meaningless, and life is on hold. However, the truth is that the time you spend in prison is still yours and holds great value if you choose to use it wisely. Even in prison, time remains life—it can be an opportunity to learn, reflect, and work on yourself.

Time as an Opportunity

Every day, every hour, and every minute you spend in prison is an opportunity for change. It's time that you can use to grow, understand yourself better, and build an improved version of yourself. While you may not have control over where you are right now, you can control how you choose to use your time. Instead of viewing each day as something to simply endure, you can see it as a gift—an opportunity to transform your life from within.

The value of time lies in what we do with it. Even in the most limited circumstances, there's always something we can do to move forward, even if it's just a small step. Using your time to learn, reflect on the past, and create a different future is the best way to make every moment in prison count.

Learn and Grow

One of the best ways to use your time in prison is through learning. Education is a powerful tool that allows you to gain new knowledge and expand your mind. You can learn through books, courses, or even by talking to others who have different experiences. Learning a new skill, a trade, or even something you've always been interested in is a way to use your time to grow and prepare for the future.

Learning not only helps you gain practical knowledge but also builds your self-confidence. Every new thing you learn is a reminder that you are capable and that you can change your life. Time in prison doesn't have to be wasted; on the contrary, it can be the time when you grow the most, discover yourself the most, and prepare the most for a better future.

Reflect and Rediscover Yourself

Time in prison is also an opportunity for reflection. In the busyness of everyday life, we often don't take the time to truly think about our decisions, our actions, and what we want for the future. Prison, though challenging, offers a space for deep reflection that we often avoid.

Reflecting on the past isn't about punishing yourself—it's about learning. Ask yourself, "What decisions brought me here?" and, more importantly, "What do I want to change moving forward?" Use this time to understand yourself better, rediscover your values, and define the kind of person you want to be. This self-awareness is one of the most valuable things you can gain from the time you have.

Work on Yourself

Time in prison can also be used to work on yourself. No matter what circumstances led you here, you always have the power to decide who you want to be from this point forward. Working on yourself means taking care of your physical, mental, and emotional health. Exercise, learning to manage stress, practicing patience, cultivating empathy, and strengthening your social skills are all ways to grow and become a better version of yourself.

Every small effort counts. Regular exercise strengthens your body and clears your mind, while meditation or deep breathing helps manage stress and anxiety. Writing or expressing your emotions enhances emotional well-being. These efforts prepare you to face life with a renewed and positive mindset when the time comes to move forward.

FINAL CONSIDERATIONS

Time is life, and every moment counts, even in prison. Despite the circumstances, the time you spend in prison is valuable, and you can choose to use it to learn, reflect, and work on yourself. Each day is an opportunity to move forward, grow, and prepare for a different and better future. Even in prison, your life is still yours, and the time you have is a gift that you can use to build a stronger, wiser, and more purpose-filled version of yourself.

~~~

IN PRISON, YOU CAN GRADUALLY BECOME AN ENHANCED VERSION OF YOURSELF

Prison can feel like a place where everything stops, where dreams are put on hold, and the future seems uncertain. However, the truth is that every day offers the opportunity to improve, to work on yourself, and to grow. It's not about ignoring your current reality but about recognizing that even in the most challenging circumstances, growth is possible. With patience and effort, it's possible to build an advanced version of yourself—one that is stronger, wiser, and more resilient. Every step, no matter how small, adds up and prepares you for the life you want to live outside. Despite the circumstances, you can improve each day by developing positive habits and skills that will help you become better and create a future filled with hope and purpose.

Improvement Happens Gradually: Patience Is Key

True change doesn't happen overnight; it's built step by step, with patience and consistency. In prison, it can be easy to feel like time stands still or that there's little you can do to improve. However, even in that environment, every small step counts. Each time you choose to do something positive for yourself, learn something new, or adopt a healthy habit, you're building a more advanced version of yourself.

The key is to be patient with yourself and recognize that change takes time. Self-improvement isn't a race; it's a continuous process that unfolds day by day. With every small effort, you get closer to the stronger, wiser version of yourself that you aspire to be.

Develop Positive Habits

One of the most important steps to improving yourself is developing positive habits that help you grow. Reading is one of the best ways to do this. It allows you to learn new things, expand your mind, and see the world from different perspectives. You can start by reading about topics that interest you, personal development, history, or even fiction that inspires you. Reading keeps your mind active and reminds you that there's always something new to learn.

Physical exercise is another positive habit that has a significant impact on your well-being. You don't need a gym to take care of your body; simple exercises can help you stay fit and relieve tension. Exercise not only improves your physical health but also has a positive effect on your mood, helping you feel stronger and more in control of your life.

Emotional and Social Skills

Working on your emotional and social skills is also essential to building an advanced version of yourself. Prison is a challenging environment, and learning to manage your emotions in a healthy way can make a big difference. Patience, empathy, and the ability to handle anger are skills you can develop gradually. Start by learning to recognize your emotions, understand what triggers them, and respond more positively.

Communication is another important skill. Learning to communicate effectively, listen to others, and express your feelings clearly and respectfully will help you build better relationships with those around you. Working on these emotional and social skills will not only help you during your time in prison but also serve as essential tools for success when you regain your freedom.

Every Small Effort Matters

It's important to remember that every small effort counts. You don't need to make big changes all at once; every small improvement is a step forward. It can be as simple as dedicating a few minutes each day to reflecting on how you feel, practicing meditation to calm your mind, or writing in a journal about your thoughts and goals. These small steps, when done consistently, have the power to transform your life in meaningful ways.

Working on yourself takes effort, but it's the best investment you can make. Every day that you choose to improve, to learn something new, or to develop a skill, you're getting closer to the advanced version of yourself that you want to be.

FINAL CONSIDERATIONS

Even in prison, you have the power to build an advanced version of yourself—gradually, with patience and effort. Developing positive habits like reading and exercising, working on your emotional and social skills, and recognizing that every small effort matters are the keys to improving day by day. Prison doesn't have to be a place where time is wasted; it can be a space where you find the courage to transform yourself, becoming stronger, wiser, and more resilient. Always remember that every day is a new opportunity to move forward and build a better version of yourself.

~~~

SERVING YOUR SENTENCE: A NEW BEGINNING WITH FREEDOM AND NO DEBTS

The journey you walk during your time in prison can be challenging, filled with ups and downs, moments of reflection, and learning. But there is something crucial to remember: once you have served your sentence, you will have paid your debt to society. That moment is where the past can be left behind, and a new opportunity arises to start fresh, free from guilt and ready to write a new chapter in your life. This new beginning is not just about starting from scratch; it's about embracing the lessons learned and using them as a foundation for a stronger, more purposeful future. Here, we will reflect on the power of that new beginning and how you can prepare to make the most of it.

Clearing the Debt: A Fresh Start

When you enter prison, a debt to society is established—a period to account for mistakes and reflect on their impact. The good news is that this debt has an endpoint. By completing your sentence, you'll have paid for what you've done and demonstrated your willingness to face the consequences. At that point, you owe nothing to anyone, marking the beginning of a fresh opportunity.

It's essential to remember that your past does not have to define who you will become in the future. Once your time is served, you have every right to seek a new life, to start fresh, and to live with dignity and without guilt. This is your chance to leave behind the weight of the past and build something new—something that reflects the best version of yourself.

Freedom to Write a New Chapter

Being released from prison means having the opportunity to write a new chapter in your life. It's the moment to decide what kind of life you want to lead and what kind of person you want to be. You have the ability to create a future full of meaning, and while the road ahead may seem difficult, remember that you have the strength and power to achieve it. Each day is a blank page, and you hold the pen to write whatever you want on it.

Think about the lessons you've learned during your time in prison. Every difficult moment, every mistake, and every reflection can be the foundation upon which you build a different and better future. These experiences, though challenging, have given you valuable insights and strength that can guide your next steps. Don't let guilt or regrets from the past define you once you've served your sentence. That chapter is over; now you have the freedom to write a new one filled with hope, growth, and opportunity, proving that change is always possible.

Prepare for the Future

Being released from prison is a new opportunity, but it's essential to be prepared to make the most of it. While serving your sentence, you can begin laying the groundwork for that fresh start. Learn as much as you can, develop new skills, work on your emotional and mental well-being, and strengthen your character. Everything you do now will help you be better prepared for the moment you regain your freedom.

Work on your personal relationships. Think about the people you want close to you and how you can contribute positively to their lives. Reconnect with your values and define your goals for the future. What do you want to achieve? How do you wish to contribute to society? These are questions you can begin answering to outline the path you want to follow.

Free from Guilt, Full of Determination

One of the most important things to remember is that once you've served your sentence, you have the right to live without guilt. You've fulfilled what society asked of you, and now it's time to focus on yourself—your dreams and your purpose. Don't let the stigma of the past hold you back. Guilt and regret can be heavy burdens, but you've settled your debt, and now it's time to free yourself from those burdens and move forward with determination.

Walk with your head held high, recognizing that the past no longer holds power over you. You are free to build a different life, create opportunities, and prove to yourself and others that change is possible. Society owes you a second chance, and you owe it to yourself as well.

FINAL CONSIDERATIONS

When you complete your sentence, you owe nothing to anyone. You've paid your debt to society, and that gives you the opportunity to begin again—free from guilt and with the ability to write a new chapter in your life. Use each day you have to prepare for this new beginning, and always remember that your past does not define you. It is your decisions today and tomorrow that truly matter. Life offers you a new opportunity, and you have the power to make the most of it.

~~~

THE POWER OF FORGIVENESS AND RECONCILIATION: A PATH TO INNER PEACE

Forgiveness is a simple word, but its power is immense. Forgiving is not easy, and sometimes it's even harder to forgive yourself. However, forgiveness is a crucial step toward inner peace and rebuilding your life. For those in prison, where the weight of past mistakes often looms heavily, forgiveness becomes a gateway to emotional freedom. Today, let's explore the value of forgiveness and reconciliation and how they can help transform your life from within.

Forgive Yourself

Forgiving yourself can be one of the hardest acts, but it is also one of the most necessary for moving forward. Everyone makes mistakes, but dwelling constantly on regret doesn't change the past—it only increases suffering. Forgiving yourself doesn't mean excusing your mistakes; it means accepting that you erred and recognizing that now you have the opportunity to learn from those mistakes and become better. It's about acknowledging your humanity and your ability to change and grow.

Self-forgiveness allows you to release the heavy burden of guilt. It's the first step toward a new version of yourself—one that is willing to learn, improve, and not let the past dictate your future. Each day is an opportunity to start anew, and forgiveness is the key to opening that door.

Forgive Others

Just as it's essential to forgive yourself, it's equally important to forgive others. Perhaps someone hurt you, life feels unfair, or others let you down. However, resentment and hatred only add to your suffering and keep you tied to the past. Forgiving others doesn't mean forgetting or excusing their actions—it's about freeing yourself from the emotional burden those feelings create. Forgiving others is a way to unshackle your heart and live in peace without letting past pain control you.

Forgiving is also an act of courage. It takes strength to let go of bitterness and allow love and compassion to take its place. By forgiving, you give yourself the gift of tranquility. You no longer allow what others did to dictate your inner peace.

Reconciliation as a Path to Healing

Forgiveness and reconciliation are closely linked. Reconciliation doesn't always mean restoring relationships with those who hurt you; sometimes, it simply means reaching a point of peace with the past and with the people who were part of it. It's about accepting what happened, learning from it, and moving forward without letting those wounds remain open.

Reconciliation can also be with yourself. You may feel like you've let yourself down, that you didn't live up to your own expectations. Reconciling with yourself means accepting your mistakes, learning from them, and committing to being better in the future. It's an act of self-love that allows you to move forward with a peaceful heart.

Strategies to Practice Forgiveness and Reconciliation

– **Acknowledge the Pain:** To forgive, you first need to recognize the pain. Take time to reflect on what happened, how it made you feel, and how it has impacted your life. Recognizing the pain is the first step to releasing it.

– **Understand Our Shared Humanity:** Nobody is perfect, and everyone makes mistakes. Understanding that even those who hurt us may be struggling with their own battles helps foster compassion.

– **Release Resentment:** Resentment is a weight that only harms you. Forgiving doesn't mean saying what happened was right—it means choosing to free yourself from the burden of resentment. Let go of bitterness and open yourself to a lighter life.

– **Focus on the Present:** Forgiveness allows you to let go of the past and focus on the present. By releasing resentment, you create space for positive things in your life. Focus your energy on what you can do today to find happiness and grow.

– **Write Down Your Feelings:** Expressing your feelings in words can be liberating. Write about your mistakes, about what others did, and about how you feel. This helps you process those emotions and find release.

– **Meditate and Reflect:** Take time for quiet reflection and connect with yourself. Meditation can help calm your mind and find the peace needed to forgive.

– **Talk to Someone You Trust:** Sharing your feelings with someone you trust can be very helpful. Talking about your mistakes and emotions helps you process them and gain support on the path to forgiveness.

The Benefits of Forgiveness

Forgiveness improves our well-being by reducing stress and creating inner peace. It helps strengthen relationships, encourages a positive outlook, and promotes peace over conflict. Additionally, it frees us from the past and from negative feelings, enabling us to move forward with clarity and purpose.

FINAL CONSIDERATIONS

Forgiveness and reconciliation are key steps toward inner peace and rebuilding your life. Forgiving yourself, forgiving others, and reconciling with the past are acts of courage that allow you to let go of resentment and move forward with lightness. Even in challenging circumstances, the power of forgiveness resides within you and can transform your life. Remember, each day is a new opportunity to choose peace, love, and growth.

~~~

THE IMPORTANCE OF GRATITUDE: FINDING LIGHT IN DIFFICULT TIMES

Life is full of challenges, especially during difficult moments like being in prison. It's easy to fall into despair and lose sight of everything we still have, everything we can be grateful for. However, even in the face of adversity, there are always reasons for gratitude. Cultivating this feeling can transform our attitude and the way we face problems, helping us find strength where we thought none existed. Gratitude reminds us of the small joys and hidden lessons in each day. Here, we will talk about the importance of gratitude and how this powerful feeling can help you develop a more positive outlook, even in the most challenging circumstances.

What is Gratitude?

Gratitude is the ability to recognize and appreciate the good things in life, no matter how small they may seem. It doesn't mean ignoring difficulties or pretending everything is fine, but focusing our attention on what brings us peace, joy, or comfort, however minor it might appear. Gratitude isn't just saying "thank you," but truly feeling it—acknowledging what we have and valuing it deeply.

In a difficult context like prison, gratitude might feel distant. But the truth is, there is always something to be thankful for: health, the support of a loved one, a meaningful conversation, or simply the opportunity to learn and grow each new day. These small moments allow us to find light even in the darkest places.

Gratitude as a Tool for Transformation

Cultivating gratitude profoundly impacts our perspective on life and our attitude. When we choose to focus on what we have instead of what we lack, we shift our outlook and strengthen our ability to face adversity. Gratitude helps us see that, despite mistakes and challenges, there are still valuable things in our lives worth appreciating.

Gratitude also connects us with others. When we recognize the support we've received and appreciate the help or words of encouragement, we strengthen our relationships and foster an environment of mutual respect. Gratitude creates a positive cycle, enabling us to maintain a hopeful and growth-oriented mindset.

Practicing Gratitude in Difficult Times

- **Find Something Positive Every Day:** Every day holds something positive, no matter how small. It could be a moment of peace, an honest conversation, or simply being alive with another opportunity to grow. Take a moment each day to reflect on something you're grateful for. Writing these moments in a gratitude journal can help you maintain a positive attitude and remember the good in your life.

– **Express Gratitude to Others:** Recognizing the positive impact others have on our lives is a powerful way to cultivate gratitude. It could be a friend, a family member, or someone who supported you during a tough time. Expressing thanks strengthens relationships and reminds us we are not alone.

– **Appreciate the Little Things:** Gratitude isn't always about grand achievements or extraordinary events. It's about appreciating the small things: a ray of sunshine, fresh air, the taste of a simple meal. Learning to value these small details trains our minds to focus on the positive and find joy in the everyday.

How Gratitude Improves Your Attitude

Practicing gratitude has a transformative effect on our attitude. When we choose gratitude, we view life from a more positive perspective. It allows us to focus on what we have instead of lamenting what we lack. This mindset gives us strength, helps us face challenges with greater calm, and enables us to maintain hope even in the darkest times.

Gratitude also reduces stress and anxiety. By focusing on the positive, we diminish the power of negative thoughts and create a healthier mental space. It shifts our perspective, enabling us to see challenges as opportunities for growth rather than obstacles. Feeling grateful connects us to the present, helps us leave behind the weight of the past, and lessens worry about the future. It fosters a sense of contentment and reminds us of the abundance that already exists in our lives. Gratitude allows us to enjoy what we have today, embrace life's small joys, and find peace in the moment.

FINAL CONSIDERATIONS

Gratitude is a powerful tool for finding light in difficult times and cultivating a positive attitude toward adversity. Even in challenging circumstances, there is always something to be thankful for. Practicing gratitude helps us appreciate the good, connect with others, and strengthen our resilience. Today, I invite you to take a moment to reflect on what you're grateful for and allow that feeling of gratitude to transform your life, filling it with hope and positivity.

~~~

HOW TO FACE STIGMA AND DISCRIMINATION: BUILDING RESILIENCE AND WALKING WITH DIGNITY

Reentering society after serving time in prison is a moment filled with hope and opportunities. However, it also comes with challenges, such as facing social stigma and discrimination. People who have served their sentences often encounter societal judgment, making reintegration and starting anew more difficult. Despite this, it is possible to approach this situation with resilience and positivity. Today, I want to share some strategies to help you face stigma and discrimination and move toward a future filled with dignity and possibility.

Acknowledging Stigma

Social stigma manifests as negative judgments toward those who have been incarcerated. It can come in the form of looks, hurtful comments, or challenges finding employment or housing. Recognizing the existence of stigma is the first step to learning how to confront it. It's important to understand that this judgment often stems from ignorance or fear. While you can't always change how others think, you can change how you respond and choose to face it.

Stigma doesn't define who you are or what you're capable of achieving. You are more than your past mistakes, and you have the power to change and create a new life. By understanding that stigma is an external perception, you can focus on what truly matters—your personal growth, well-being, and the future you want to build.

Build Emotional Resilience

One key to dealing with stigma and discrimination is to develop emotional resilience. Resilience allows you to stay strong in the face of adversity and move forward despite obstacles. This includes learning to manage the negative emotions that may arise from rejection.

A powerful way to build resilience is by reflecting on everything you've already overcome. Think about the challenges you've faced and the strength you've demonstrated. Every obstacle you've surmounted proves your ability to adapt and persevere. Focusing on your capacity to overcome hardships will empower you to face stigma with a positive and determined attitude.

Surround Yourself with Supportive People

Having people who believe in you can make a significant difference in your reintegration process. Surround yourself with friends, family, and organizations that encourage you to keep moving forward. These individuals can offer encouragement, guide you during tough times, and help you maintain a positive perspective.

Seek support groups or communities that work with people in similar situations. These organizations often consist of individuals who understand what you're going through and can provide resources and emotional support. Being around people who understand and support you can be a powerful source of strength for facing stigma and confidently moving forward.

Focus on What You Can Control

You can't control what others think of you, but you can control how you react and what you choose to do. Instead of focusing on others' judgments, concentrate on actions that improve your situation and help you build the life you want. This includes working on your personal development, learning new skills, finding employment, and maintaining a positive outlook.

Show through your actions that you've changed and are committed to a new beginning. Sometimes, the best way to combat stigma is through deeds: demonstrating with your decisions and behavior that you're a different person and willing to make positive contributions to society.

Don't Let Stigma Define You

Stigma might make you feel unworthy or incapable of change, but that's a false perception. Don't define yourself by your past mistakes or by others' negative opinions. You are more than your errors, and you have the power to decide who you want to be moving forward.

Always remember that you are a person of value, with talents and the ability to make a difference. Every day is an opportunity to grow, learn, and build a life of dignity. Don't let stigma limit your potential or make you doubt what you can achieve. Focus on your strengths, what you've learned, and the future you want to create.

FINAL CONSIDERATIONS

Facing stigma and discrimination after leaving prison isn't easy, but it is possible to approach it with resilience and positivity. Recognize that stigma doesn't define who you are or what you can achieve. Build emotional resilience, surround yourself with supportive people, focus on what you can control, and don't let others' judgment limit your potential. You have the power to write a new story and prove that change is possible. Walk with your head held high, with dignity, and with the conviction that you are much more than your past.

~~~

STRESS AND ANXIETY MANAGEMENT: STRATEGIES TO FIND CALM IN DIFFICULT TIMES

Life in prison can be deeply stressful. Restrictions, uncertainty about the future, loneliness, and daily challenges can lead to high levels of anxiety. However, even in these circumstances, it is possible to find ways to manage stress and regain a sense of calm. Today, I want to share some effective strategies for managing stress and anxiety while in prison, using techniques like deep breathing, meditation, exercise, and mindfulness.

Understanding Stress and Anxiety

Stress and anxiety are natural responses to challenging situations. When under pressure, our bodies react with a "fight or flight" response, preparing us to face the perceived threat. However, when these responses are constantly activated, they can negatively impact physical and mental well-being, leading to exhaustion or chronic health issues over time. Feeling stressed or anxious is not a sign of weakness; it's a natural reaction to a tough environment and a reminder that we need to find healthy ways to cope and adapt.

The key is learning to manage these emotions to reduce their impact and maintain a clearer and more focused mind.

Techniques to Manage Stress and Anxiety

1. Deep Breathing

This is one of the most effective techniques for reducing stress. When stressed, our breathing becomes rapid and shallow. Practicing deep breathing helps calm the nervous system and sends a signal to the brain that everything is okay.

How to Practice It:

– Find a quiet spot and sit comfortably.

– Inhale deeply through your nose for 4 seconds, hold your breath for 4 seconds, and exhale slowly through your mouth for 6–8 seconds.

– Repeat this cycle several times, focusing on the rhythm of your breathing.

2. Meditation

Meditation calms the mind and focuses attention on the present. It doesn't require much time or special equipment—just a few minutes a day can bring inner peace.

How to Get Started:

- Sit in a quiet place, close your eyes, and focus on your breath.

- If your mind starts to wander, gently bring your focus back to your breath.

- Start with short sessions of 5–10 minutes and gradually increase the duration.

3. Physical Exercise

Exercise releases endorphins, the "happiness hormones," which help reduce stress and improve mood.

Practical Options in Prison:

- Do simple exercises like push-ups, squats, sit-ups, or walking in available spaces.

- Dedicate 20–30 minutes daily to a simple physical routine to feel the benefits.

4. Mindfulness

Mindfulness involves paying full attention to the present without judgment. It helps reduce anxiety by focusing on the "here and now."

How to Integrate It Into Your Day:

- Pay attention to physical sensations, the sounds around you, or the taste of your food.

- The key is to be fully present in whatever you're doing, without distractions.

Create a Routine to Reduce Stress

Incorporating these techniques into a daily routine provides a sense of control and structure, which are essential for emotional well-being. Start your day with breathing exercises or meditation, dedicate time to physical activity, and practice mindfulness throughout the day. Consistency is key to experiencing positive changes in your mood and overall well-being.

FINAL CONSIDERATIONS

Stress and anxiety are natural responses, but they don't have to control your life. With techniques like deep breathing, meditation, exercise, and mindfulness, you can manage these emotions and find calm even in challenging environments like prison. Establishing a daily routine that includes these practices will help reduce the impact of stress, strengthen your mind, and maintain a positive outlook. While you may not be able to change your current circumstances, you can decide how to face them.

~~~

IMPORTANCE OF EDUCATION AND LIFELONG LEARNING: A DRIVER FOR CHANGE AND OPPORTUNITIES

Education has the power to transform lives and open doors to new opportunities, especially when starting over. It not only provides knowledge but also the confidence to face challenges and adapt to new circumstances. Regardless of where you are in life, continuous learning can be a powerful tool for personal growth and building a brighter future. Education empowers you to see beyond your current limitations, inspiring you to take steps toward your goals. Here, we will talk about the importance of education—both formal and informal—and how it can drive change in your life, opening new doors and uncovering possibilities.

Education as a Tool for Transformation

Education goes beyond what you learn in a classroom or the pursuit of a diploma. It's a tool that helps us better understand the world, develop skills, and find new ways to solve problems. Education changes our mindset, helps us make better decisions, and leads to a more fulfilling life.

For those who have spent time in prison, education can serve as a bridge to a new life. Learning a new skill, earning a diploma, or simply acquiring knowledge in an area of interest can make all the difference when reintegrating into society. Education gives you the confidence to know you have something valuable to offer, which is crucial in building a new version of yourself.

Benefits of Lifelong Learning

Lifelong learning knows no age or boundaries—there's always something new to learn. Here are some key benefits:

– **Expands Employment Opportunities:** Knowledge and skills acquired through education open new career paths. Learning a trade, developing technical skills, or completing academic studies can help you secure a job and build a stable life. Often, gaining new skills makes you more competitive and provides access to jobs that once seemed out of reach.

– **Builds Confidence and Self-Esteem:** Learning doesn't just provide knowledge; it boosts your confidence. Acquiring new skills proves to yourself that you can overcome challenges and grow. This confidence is essential for facing future challenges with courage and for believing in your ability to achieve your goals.

– **Enhances Adaptability:** The world is constantly changing, and adaptability is essential for success. Education and lifelong learning keep you updated and ready to meet new demands in the job market and society. The more you learn, the better prepared you are to face change and seize opportunities.

– **Improves Social and Communication Skills:** Education isn't just about technical knowledge—it also helps develop social and communication skills. Through learning, you improve your ability to express ideas, listen to others, and build effective relationships. These skills are crucial for fostering healthy relationships and succeeding in any field.

Options for Education and Lifelong Learning

Education doesn't have to be formal; there are many ways to keep learning and growing, even without access to traditional schools or universities. Here are some options:

– **Educational Programs in Prison:** Many prisons offer educational programs, ranging from basic classes to vocational training. Participating in these programs is a great way to use your time and prepare for the future. If you have the chance, enroll in courses that interest you or align with your future goals.

– **Reading and Self-Learning:** Reading is a powerful tool for learning. You can find books on a wide range of topics, from practical skills to personal development. Reading allows you to learn at your own pace and explore subjects that interest you. Additionally, self-learning through books, magazines, or educational videos is an effective way to keep growing.

– **Online Courses:** If you have internet access, online courses are a fantastic way to learn. Many platforms offer free or affordable courses on various topics, from technical skills to personal development. Utilizing these resources can help you acquire useful competencies for reintegration into society.

Commitment to Learning

Lifelong learning requires commitment and perseverance. It may feel challenging or frustrating, especially when you don't see immediate results, but every small step brings you closer to your goals. Commit to learning something new each day, whether through reading, attending a course, or talking to someone who has knowledge you lack.

Learning will not only help you build a better life for yourself but also allow you to inspire those around you who are seeking change. Education is a powerful tool to transform not only your life but also the environment you're in.

FINAL CONSIDERATIONS

Education and lifelong learning are drivers for change and opportunities. No matter where you are in life, there's always something new to learn and always a chance to grow. Take every opportunity to learn, whether formally or informally, and commit to becoming the best version of yourself. Learning is the key that will unlock new doors and allow you to create the future you desire.

~~~

LIFE AND WORK SKILLS POST-INCARCERATION: BUILDING A PRODUCTIVE AND MOTIVATED FUTURE

Leaving prison marks the beginning of a new phase filled with opportunities and challenges. To successfully reintegrate into society, it is crucial to acquire practical skills for both daily life and the workplace. These skills will not only make you more independent and productive but also help you build a future with purpose and stability. They serve as the foundation for personal growth, allowing you to navigate your new path with confidence and resilience. Here, we will explore essential life and work skills to help you take your first steps toward a fulfilling and motivating life.

Life Skills for Everyday Living

Adapting to life after prison can be challenging, but practical skills can help you become more independent and successful. Key life skills include:

– **Money Management and Personal Finances:** Learning to handle money is essential for living independently and avoiding financial problems. This includes budgeting, saving, and effectively managing your income. Creating a monthly budget can help you control spending and save for the future. Understanding basic concepts like saving, avoiding debt, and limiting unnecessary expenses is a key life skill.

– **Decision-Making:** Making sound decisions is critical for navigating daily life. This involves evaluating your options, considering potential consequences, and choosing the best course of action. Strong decision-making skills can lead to a stable life and help you avoid falling back into negative patterns.

– **Problem-Solving:** Life is full of challenges, and being able to address them effectively is vital. Problem-solving skills involve analyzing the situation, exploring alternatives, and selecting the best solution. Staying proactive and focusing on solutions rather than problems will help you face challenges confidently.

– **Effective Communication:** Communication is essential for building healthy relationships and navigating any environment. Learning to express yourself clearly, listen actively, and respect others' opinions will help you foster positive relationships with loved ones, coworkers, and employers. Effective communication also enables peaceful and constructive conflict resolution.

Workplace Skills for a Successful Future

Employment is one of the most important aspects of a successful reintegration. Having a job not only provides financial stability but also instills a sense of purpose. Key workplace skills include:

– **Technical Skills:** Technical skills are necessary for performing specific job tasks. Learning a trade or developing technical competencies can open new job opportunities. Skills like carpentry, electrical work, machinery repair, gardening, or cooking are valuable and often accessible through courses or workshops, even in prison.

– **Job Search Skills:** Finding a job can be challenging, but certain skills can make the process easier. Learn how to craft a resume that highlights your skills and experience, practice for job interviews, and develop a positive attitude. Perseverance is essential—don't be discouraged by rejections; keep searching until you find the right opportunity.

– **Teamwork:** The ability to work well with others is highly valued in any workplace. Teamwork involves collaboration, respecting diverse perspectives, and contributing to shared goals. Demonstrating respect and a willingness to assist others is key to creating a positive work environment and standing out as a reliable employee.

– **Time Management and Responsibility:** Punctuality and fulfilling assigned responsibilities are fundamental for maintaining a job. Time management involves organizing daily activities to meet commitments without feeling overwhelmed. Being responsible and completing tasks on time will earn the trust of your employers and help you maintain job stability.

Preparing for a Hopeful Future

Acquiring life and work skills will not only improve your quality of life but also boost your confidence and help you envision a future full of possibilities. Use your time in prison to learn as much as you can through educational programs, workshops, or even by sharing knowledge with fellow inmates. Every skill you develop brings you closer to the life you want to build after regaining your freedom.

No matter how difficult the past has been, there is always a path forward if you choose to take it. Work on personal growth, continue learning, and prepare to seize the opportunities that lie ahead. With life and work skills, you'll face the future with greater confidence and determination, building a fulfilling and purposeful life.

FINAL CONSIDERATIONS

Life and work skills are essential for a successful reintegration after prison. Learning to manage money, make sound decisions, solve problems, and communicate effectively are critical for everyday life, while developing technical skills, searching for jobs, and working well with others are vital for the workplace. Remember that every skill you acquire will help you build a better future, and the effort you put in today will bring you closer to the life you envision for tomorrow.

~~~

DEVELOPING SOCIAL AND COMMUNICATION SKILLS: THE KEY TO SUCCESSFUL REINTEGRATION

Reintegrating into society after time in prison is a challenge that goes beyond finding a job or rebuilding daily life. It requires the ability to interact with others, build healthy relationships, and actively participate in the community. It also involves rebuilding trust, both in yourself and with those around you, which can be a gradual but rewarding process. Developing social and communication skills is essential to connect with others positively and authentically. Let's explore strategies to enhance these skills and how they can be your foundation for successful reintegration, meaningful relationships, and a fulfilling sense of belonging.

The Importance of Social and Communication Skills

Social skills enable us to interact effectively with those around us. They include listening, expressing thoughts and emotions clearly, empathizing, and resolving conflicts peacefully. These abilities are crucial not only for maintaining healthy relationships but also for navigating the workplace and contributing to the community.

Effective communication is the foundation of all human relationships. Knowing how to express your ideas respectfully and clearly while actively listening and understanding others is vital for building positive connections. Effective communication helps avoid misunderstandings, resolve conflicts, and show respect and commitment to others.

Strategies to Develop Social and Communication Skills

1. Practice Active Listening

Active listening goes beyond hearing words; it involves understanding what the other person is truly conveying through words and body language. It means focusing, avoiding interruptions, and asking questions to show interest.

Practical Tip: Maintain eye contact, nod occasionally, and ask follow-up questions to demonstrate you're paying attention. This strengthens relationships and makes the other person feel valued.

2. Express Your Feelings and Needs Clearly

Clear and assertive expression is essential for effective communication. Assertiveness allows you to communicate honestly without aggression, respecting both your needs and those of others.

Practical Tip: Use "I" statements to express your feelings. For example, say, "I feel frustrated when this happens" instead of "You always mess up." This avoids making the other person feel attacked and fosters open conversation.

3. Practice Empathy

Empathy is the ability to put yourself in someone else's shoes and understand their emotions. It helps you connect better with others and build meaningful relationships.

Practical Tip: When someone shares a problem or feeling, try to see things from their perspective. Use phrases like, "I can see how that would be hard for you," to show understanding and support.

4. Learn Conflict Resolution Skills

Conflicts are inevitable, but how you handle them makes all the difference. Learning to resolve conflicts peacefully and constructively is an essential social skill.

Practical Tip: Focus on solving the issue rather than "winning" the argument. Ask, "How can we work this out together?" and strive for a solution that benefits both parties.

5. Improve Your Body Language

Communication isn't just verbal; body language, facial expressions, and tone of voice also convey messages. A genuine smile, steady eye contact, or an open posture can make your message more impactful and trustworthy. Ensure that your nonverbal communication aligns with your words to create clarity and strengthen your interactions.

Practical Tip: Maintain an open posture, avoid crossing your arms, and make eye contact to show interest and confidence. Smiling and using a calm tone of voice create a positive atmosphere in conversations.

Daily Practice and Reflection

Developing social and communication skills requires daily practice and self-reflection. Don't be discouraged if it feels challenging at first—every interaction is an opportunity to learn and improve. Reflect on your communication after each interaction and consider what you could do differently next time.

Observe individuals you admire as good communicators. Learn how they express themselves, listen, and handle conflicts. Modeling their behaviors can help you build your own skills and become more effective in your interactions.

FINAL CONSIDERATIONS

Developing social and communication skills is crucial for successful reintegration. Practicing active listening, expressing your feelings assertively, showing empathy, resolving conflicts, and being mindful of your body language will help you build healthier and more meaningful relationships. Effective communication not only benefits your personal life but also enhances your professional and community involvement, leading to a more fulfilling and connected life.

~~~

THE VALUE OF CONTRIBUTION AND SERVICE: FINDING PURPOSE THROUGH SUPPORTING OTHERS

One of the biggest challenges for people in prison is the feeling of a lack of purpose and connection to the community. The environment can feel isolating, leading to the belief that there's nothing valuable one can contribute. However, even within the confines of prison, every person has the ability to contribute and become a source of support for others. Acts of kindness, mentorship, or simply offering a listening ear can create a ripple effect of positivity and hope. Let's explore the immense value of contribution and service to others, and how these acts can provide purpose and meaning, even in difficult circumstances, helping to foster a sense of belonging and personal growth.

The Power of Contribution

Contributing to a community and helping others are powerful ways to bring purpose to life. Contribution connects us with others and helps us feel part of something bigger, giving us a sense of value and the ability to make a positive impact. While it may seem that contributing is only possible outside prison, there are many ways to support others even within a confined environment.

Helping another person—whether by sharing knowledge, offering words of encouragement, or simply listening—creates a ripple of positive impact, benefiting both the giver and the receiver. Contribution fosters satisfaction, belonging, and purpose, turning a challenging situation into an opportunity for growth and positive influence.

Ways to Contribute While in Prison

1. Emotional Support for Peers

Sometimes, the most meaningful way to help is simply being present and offering emotional support. Prison can be a lonely place, and many people face moments of distress or hopelessness. Being a source of encouragement, listening without judgment, and offering kind words can make a profound difference in someone's life.

2. Sharing Knowledge

Everyone has unique skills or knowledge to share. Perhaps you know gardening, carpentry, math, or literacy that you could teach to others. Sharing your abilities not only helps others grow but also gives you a sense of purpose and personal satisfaction. By offering your knowledge, you create connections, build a supportive community, and reinforce your own learning in the process, strengthening your sense of accomplishment.

3. Participating in Community Activities

Many prisons offer community-based programs or activities. These initiatives benefit both the internal community and, sometimes, the external community as well. Getting involved in these programs allows you to contribute tangibly and to feel part of something positive and meaningful.

4. Supporting Daily Responsibilities

Inside prison, there are daily tasks that ensure everyone's well-being. Taking part in cleaning, helping in the kitchen, or assisting with other daily activities is a way to serve the community and contribute to the collective good.

Benefits of Contributing to Others

Contributing to others offers numerous benefits for both the giver and the recipient. By focusing on what you can do rather than on limitations, you shift your mindset towards positivity and agency. This change in perspective helps reduce stress and anxiety while fostering a sense of usefulness and connection.

Contribution also helps you build social and emotional skills such as empathy, communication, and patience. These skills are invaluable for reintegration into society, aiding in building healthier relationships and adapting to new environments.

Moreover, serving others allows you to become a positive influence, showing that despite past mistakes, you are capable of doing good and making a difference.

Finding Purpose and a Sense of Belonging

Contributing to the community fosters a sense of belonging. Helping others makes you realize that you are part of something bigger, that your life has an impact, and that you can make a difference. This sense of belonging provides purpose—a reason to strive each day, motivating you to improve and keep moving forward.

Contribution also helps change the narrative you tell yourself about who you are. Instead of focusing on past mistakes, you can focus on the good you are doing now. This shift in perspective is essential for building a new identity and gaining confidence in your ability to reintegrate into society positively and meaningfully.

FINAL CONSIDERATIONS

The value of contribution and service to others is immeasurable. Even in a challenging environment like prison, there are always ways to help, support, and make a difference. Contribution allows you to find purpose, reduce stress, develop skills, and feel connected to something greater. Seek ways to contribute to your community, become a source of support for others, and find purpose and belonging through the act of service. Remember, every positive action you take today lays the foundation for a meaningful and purposeful tomorrow.

~~~

REBUILDING RELATIONSHIPS WITH LOVED ONES: HEALING BONDS AND RECONNECTING

Life in prison not only impacts the individual serving time but also profoundly affects their loved ones—parents, children, partners, siblings, and friends. Relationships can become strained or even broken due to the pain, distance, and challenges that arise during this period. However, the possibility of healing and rebuilding those bonds always exists. Reintegrating into society isn't just about finding work or adapting to a new environment; it's also about reconnecting with family and friends. Let's explore how to work toward healing damaged relationships and building a new foundation of love and support with your loved ones.

Understanding Others' Pain

The first step in rebuilding relationships is recognizing the impact your absence has had on your loved ones' lives. They, too, have experienced suffering—grief, anger, confusion, or even a sense of betrayal. Acknowledging and validating these feelings is essential for beginning the process of reconciliation.

Demonstrate empathy by putting yourself in their shoes. Recognizing the pain they've endured can help open the door to dialogue and mutual healing. This act of understanding creates a shared foundation for rebuilding trust and connection.

Open Communication and Humility

Open communication is the cornerstone of repairing relationships. Speak honestly about your feelings, regrets, and hopes for the future. Apologizing for past actions can be challenging but is an essential step in healing the harm caused.

Equally important is the willingness to listen. Giving your loved ones space to express their emotions without interruption or defensiveness shows that you value their experiences and perspectives. This fosters an environment of trust and mutual understanding, essential for relationship repair.

Time and Patience: Respecting the Process

Healing relationships takes time and patience. Your loved ones may need time to process their emotions and adjust to changes. Demonstrating patience shows your commitment to the process and reassures them of your sincerity.

Understand that there may be setbacks, and progress may not always be linear. The key is to stay consistent and dedicated. Small gestures, like a thoughtful message, a heartfelt letter, or simply being present, can make a significant difference over time.

Restoring Trust

Trust is the foundation of any relationship, and if it has been broken, it must be rebuilt with consistent, genuine actions. Avoid making promises you can't keep, and follow through on your commitments. Demonstrating reliability and accountability is essential to earning back your loved ones' trust.

Creating New Experiences Together

One effective way to strengthen a relationship is by creating positive new memories. Once you regain your freedom, find opportunities to spend quality time with your loved ones, such as sharing a meal, taking a walk, or simply talking openly.

These shared moments help shift focus away from past pain and toward a hopeful future. Building new experiences allows everyone to reconnect and rediscover each other, reinforcing emotional bonds and demonstrating your commitment to being an active, supportive part of their lives.

FINAL CONSIDERATIONS

Rebuilding relationships after imprisonment is challenging but possible with empathy, open communication, patience, and a commitment to change. Trust is restored through consistent actions, and small gestures can strengthen bonds. Reintegration includes reconnecting with loved ones, proving it's never too late to heal and rebuild meaningful connections.

~~~

HOW TO MAINTAIN LONG-TERM MOTIVATION: FOCUS ON YOUR FUTURE AND AVOID FALLING BACK INTO OLD HABITS

Leaving prison marks a fresh start, full of opportunities to build a better life. However, it also comes with challenges that will test your motivation and ability to stay focused. Maintaining long-term motivation is crucial to avoid slipping back into past habits and moving forward toward a more meaningful and fulfilling life. Let's explore strategies to help you stay motivated, even when the road gets tough.

Motivation as a Daily Journey

Motivation is not something you find once and keep forever—it's something you must cultivate daily. There will be moments when you feel energized and ready to move forward, and others when your motivation seems to fade. Understanding that motivation is a journey helps you prepare for challenges and find ways to persevere, even during the difficult times.

Strategies for Maintaining Long-Term Motivation

1- Set Clear and Realistic Goals

– Define specific, achievable goals that provide direction.

– Set both long-term goals (e.g., finding a stable job or rebuilding a relationship) and short-term goals (e.g., completing a daily task or learning a new skill).

– Breaking larger goals into smaller, manageable steps helps you make progress without feeling overwhelmed.

2- Surround Yourself with Positive People

– The people around you greatly influence your mindset and motivation.

– Surround yourself with supportive individuals who encourage your growth and believe in your potential.

– Seek out friends, family, or support groups that align with your goals and provide encouragement during tough times.

3- Celebrate Your Achievements

– Acknowledge and celebrate every accomplishment, no matter how small.

– Recognizing your progress reinforces your motivation and reminds you of how far you've come.

– Keep a journal of your achievements to reflect on your growth and inspire yourself to keep going.

4- Focus on Your Purpose

– When faced with challenges or moments of doubt, reconnect with the purpose driving your actions.

– Remind yourself why you're working toward your goals, whether it's to build a better life for yourself, provide for your family, or pursue a dream.

– Spend a few minutes each day visualizing the future you want—how it will look, feel, and impact your life.

5- Learn from Failures

– Failures are part of the journey and should not discourage you.

– View setbacks as opportunities to learn and grow.

– Reflect on what went wrong, identify what you can do differently, and use those lessons to refine your approach moving forward.

6- Maintain a Positive Routine

– Create a daily routine filled with activities that promote growth and well-being.

– Include habits like exercising, meditating, reading, or developing new skills to keep yourself focused and energized.

– A consistent routine provides stability and helps you stay motivated, even in challenging circumstances.

FINAL CONSIDERATIONS

Maintaining long-term motivation after leaving prison can be challenging, but with the right strategies, it's entirely achievable. Setting clear goals, surrounding yourself with positive influences, celebrating milestones, focusing on your purpose, learning from failures, and maintaining a positive routine are essential tools to keep you moving forward. Remember, every day is a new opportunity to take a step toward the future you desire. Consistent effort and determination will lead you to achieve your dreams and avoid falling back into old habits. The path may be challenging, but your potential for growth and transformation is limitless.

~~~

NECESSARY QUESTIONS: INTROSPECTION FOR GROWTH

Being in prison doesn't mean personal development has to stop. In fact, it can be a powerful time to turn inward and reflect on ways to grow and transform. Introspection is a tool for finding clarity, peace, and motivation for the future. Here are some guiding questions to help you focus and start your introspective journey:

Reflective Questions for Growth

What mistakes have I made, and what lessons can I learn from them?

Reflecting on your mistakes isn't about destructive self-criticism—it's about uncovering lessons that can help you become better. Ask yourself how you can transform those mistakes into valuable learning experiences and avoid repeating them.

~~~

Who have I hurt, and how can I make amends with them or with myself?

Growth involves facing the pain you may have caused and finding ways to heal those relationships. This reflection can lead to inner peace and pave the way for reconciliation.

~~~

What virtues do I have, and how can I use them to improve my life and help others?

Everyone has strengths. Identifying them helps you recognize your value and consider how to use these strengths for positive change in your life and the lives of others.

~~~

What habits brought me here, and which ones can I change to create a different future?

Change begins with recognizing patterns that hold you back. Reflect on which habits hinder your growth and how you can replace them with healthier ones.

~~~

What dreams or goals do I have for the future, and how can I prepare now to achieve them?

Prison can be a time to reflect on what you want to accomplish when you regain your freedom. Having a clear vision of your goals helps align today's actions with the future you want.

~~~

What can I be grateful for today, despite my circumstances?

Practicing gratitude, even in adversity, fosters positivity and motivation. Reflect on what you do have, the people who support you, or the lessons you've learned.

~~~

How can I become a better version of myself each day?

Personal growth is a continual process. Every day offers a chance to improve upon yesterday. Consider the concrete steps you can take daily to keep growing.

~~~

What negative thoughts hold me back, and how can I replace them with positive ones?

Identifying limiting beliefs is crucial for change. Reflect on how to transform these negative thoughts into affirmations that propel you forward.

~~~

What keeps me motivated to move forward, even in tough moments?

Connecting with your deep motivations will give you strength during difficult times. Reflect on what inspires you to keep going.

~~~

How can I forgive myself for past mistakes?

Self-forgiveness is essential for growth. Reflect on how to stop punishing yourself for the past and embrace the possibility of change.

~~~

What skills or knowledge can I gain during this time to improve my future?

Use this time to learn something new. Reflect on what skills could lead to a better future and how you might start developing them.

~~~

How can I contribute positively to the prison community?

Even in prison, you can make a positive impact. Reflect on how you can support or help those around you.

~~~

How can I strengthen my resilience in the face of challenges?

Resilience is the ability to bounce back after setbacks. Reflect on how to cultivate this skill to overcome daily obstacles.

~~~

What does inner freedom mean to me, and how can I nurture it?

Freedom isn't always physical. Reflect on how to feel free internally, despite external circumstances.
~~~

~~~

What kind of person do I want to be when I regain my freedom?

Visualize the version of yourself you want to build. Reflect on the qualities, attitudes, and habits you want to embody and how you can start developing them today.

~~~

FINAL CONSIDERATIONS

Introspection is a powerful tool for personal growth. Even in difficult circumstances, there's always space to transform your inner self. Reflecting on your past, motivations, and goals gives you the clarity needed for a better future. Remember, all change starts from within.

~~~

INSPIRING STORIES: A NEW BEGINNING IS POSSIBLE

It's easy to believe that the past permanently defines our future, but the truth is that change is always within reach. Being in prison can feel like the end, but for many, it becomes the start of a profound personal transformation. History is filled with examples of individuals who turned their lives around after incarceration, proving that a new beginning is possible for anyone. Let's explore some inspiring stories that demonstrate that, no matter how difficult the past, it's always possible to build a brighter future.

Malcolm X: Transformation Through Knowledge

Malcolm X spent time in prison, where he decided to completely change his life. Immersing himself in reading, he explored history, politics, and religion, which ignited his passion for justice. He emerged as a leader for the African-American community and a powerful voice in the fight for civil rights in the United States. Malcolm X's journey shows how knowledge can be a tool for transformation, proving that growth is possible even in the most challenging circumstances.

Nelson Mandela: From Prisoner to President

Nelson Mandela's life exemplifies how adversity can shape leaders. Despite enduring harsh conditions during 27 years in prison, he maintained hope for a racially united South Africa. Mandela emerged from incarceration committed to reconciliation, not revenge, becoming the first black president of South Africa. His leadership helped transition the country toward equality and peace. His story highlights how forgiveness, resilience, and hope can transform not only a life but an entire nation.

Viktor Frankl: Finding Meaning Amid Suffering

As a Holocaust survivor, Viktor Frankl endured unimaginable suffering. During his imprisonment, he observed that those who found a sense of purpose were more likely to endure hardship. After his release, he authored *Man's Search for Meaning*, emphasizing the human capacity to find meaning even in the face of despair. Frankl's philosophy demonstrates that while circumstances may be beyond our control, the way we respond can shape our future.

Miguel de Cervantes: Creativity in Confinement

Miguel de Cervantes, the author of *Don Quixote*, spent time in prison on several occasions. It's believed that he wrote parts of his masterpiece during his incarceration. Cervantes turned his time in confinement into an opportunity to create one of the most celebrated works in literature, showing that even in challenging conditions, creativity can flourish and inspire the world.

Fyodor Dostoevsky: A Literary Rebirth

Russian novelist Fyodor Dostoevsky spent years in a Siberian prison, an experience that profoundly influenced his writing. His time in captivity deepened his reflections on human nature and morality, themes vividly portrayed in *Crime and Punishment* and *The Brothers Karamazov.* Dostoevsky's story is a testament to how adversity can lead to profound personal and creative growth.

Oscar Wilde: Redemption Through Writing

Oscar Wilde's two years in prison profoundly shaped his later works. He wrote *De Profundis*, a letter reflecting on his life and suffering, and *The Ballad of Reading Gaol*, capturing the struggles and redemption of prison life. Wilde used his art to find purpose and healing, proving that creativity can be a powerful tool for transformation.

FINAL CONSIDERATIONS

These inspiring stories remind us that a new beginning is always possible. Figures like Malcolm X, Nelson Mandela, Viktor Frankl, Miguel de Cervantes, Fyodor Dostoevsky, and Oscar Wilde found reasons to grow and contribute positively despite their circumstances. Being in prison does not define who you are or who you will become. You always have the power to change, to be better, and to work toward a brighter future. History teaches us that even in the darkest times, the light of hope and change can be ignited.

~~~

GLOSSARIES

This glossary system has been designed to delve into key concepts related to resilience, personal growth, emotional well-being, and relationship rebuilding. Its purpose is not only to clarify terms but also to inspire and provide a deeper understanding of the fundamental pillars for your process of social reintegration and personal development.

By exploring these concepts, you will gain the tools to navigate your journey with greater confidence and clarity. Each word has been carefully chosen with a clear objective: to help you build a new story—a story of freedom, redemption, and the full realization of your potential.

These words will guide you in transforming challenges into opportunities for growth and renewal, empowering you to embrace change and create a life of meaning and fulfillment.

RESILIENCE AND PERSONAL GROWTH

This glossary explores key concepts that define resilience and personal growth, offering insights to help you navigate challenges and embrace opportunities for transformation. Each term has been carefully chosen to inspire and empower you on your journey toward self-discovery, strength, and fulfillment. By understanding these ideas, you can build a foundation for thriving in the face of adversity and unlocking your true potential. These concepts will guide you in making meaningful progress, turning obstacles into stepping stones for a more empowered and purposeful life.

Acceptance: Recognizing our emotions and circumstances as they are, without judgment. Acceptance helps us stop resisting what we can't change and focus on improving what we can.

Adaptability: The ability to adjust to difficult situations or changes with flexibility, always seeking the best way to face new realities.

Self-Compassion: Treating yourself with kindness and understanding when things don't go as planned. It reduces self-criticism and encourages learning and personal growth.

Self-Confidence: Believing in your abilities to face challenges and achieve goals. It gives you the security needed to act and overcome obstacles.

Self-Discipline: The ability to control impulses and stay focused on what's important. Self-discipline helps you make decisions that benefit your well-being and growth.

Personal Growth: A continuous process of improvement to develop skills, overcome limitations, and reach your full potential.

Determination: The firmness to keep going and achieve your goals, despite difficulties. It keeps you focused on what you want to accomplish.

Empathy: The ability to put yourself in someone else's shoes and understand their emotions. Empathy helps build relationships based on respect and understanding.

Hope: Believing in a better future and working toward it. Hope motivates you to maintain a positive attitude and move toward your goals.

Optimism: The tendency to see the bright side of situations and expect good outcomes. Optimism strengthens resilience during tough times.

Patience: The ability to tolerate discomfort or delays without frustration. Patience is essential for overcoming challenges and understanding that growth takes time.

Perseverance: Persisting with effort and determination despite obstacles. Perseverance teaches you to keep going and fight for your goals.

Proactivity: Taking initiative and acting before problems arise. Proactivity helps you take control of your circumstances and anticipate challenges.

Resilience: The ability to recover from setbacks and emerge stronger. Resilience means learning from difficulties and turning them into opportunities for growth.

~~~
~~~

EMOTIONS AND MENTAL WELL-BEING

This glossary is dedicated to understanding the intricate relationship between emotions and mental well-being. Each term provides a deeper insight into the emotional states and practices that contribute to a balanced and fulfilling life.

By exploring these concepts, you can develop greater emotional intelligence, manage challenges effectively, and nurture a healthier, more resilient mindset. Moreover, understanding these emotional tools can empower you to foster stronger relationships, improve self-awareness, and enhance your overall quality of life. As you apply these principles, you will find yourself better equipped to navigate life's ups and downs with grace and confidence.

Joy: A feeling of pleasure or satisfaction that energizes you and helps maintain a positive attitude.

Anxiety: A sense of excessive worry or fear about the unknown. Understanding and managing anxiety is essential for emotional balance.

Self-Compassion: Treating yourself with kindness and understanding, especially when facing mistakes or failures. It helps reduce self-criticism and focuses on learning and growth.

Self-Confidence: Believing in your ability to face challenges and achieve goals. It drives you to act with assurance and overcome obstacles.

Compassion: The ability to feel others' pain and the desire to alleviate it. Compassion motivates you to support those in need and strengthen your relationships.

Empathy: The capacity to put yourself in someone else's shoes and understand their feelings. Empathy fosters meaningful connections and enhances relationships.

Hope: The belief that good things are ahead. Hope is the driving force that keeps you moving forward, even during tough times.

Emotional Strength: The ability to stay balanced in the face of challenges. Emotional strength helps you tackle difficulties with positivity and resilience.

Frustration: The feeling of discouragement when things don't go as planned. Learning to handle frustration helps you grow and find alternative solutions.

Gratitude: Appreciating and valuing what you have, even in difficult moments. Gratitude shifts your focus to life's positive aspects, enhancing emotional well-being.

Motivation: The internal drive to act and achieve goals. Motivation keeps you focused and helps you overcome obstacles.

Emotional Resilience: The ability to manage tough emotions and recover from adversity. It is key to maintaining mental balance during challenging times.

Serenity: A state of calm that allows you to act clearly and deliberately. Serenity is vital for managing stress and making thoughtful decisions.

Tranquility: An inner peace that helps you handle situations with clarity. Tranquility is fundamental for making sound decisions and staying composed under pressure.

Sadness: An emotion that arises in response to loss or painful experiences. Acknowledging sadness allows you to process your feelings and move toward healing.

~~~

SOCIO-EMOTIONAL SKILLS

This glossary highlights the essential socio-emotional skills needed to navigate relationships, foster personal growth, and enhance overall well-being. Each term delves into the abilities that enable effective communication, empathy, and emotional resilience. These skills are not only tools for managing challenges but also keys to building meaningful relationships and a positive self-image. By mastering these skills, you can build stronger connections, manage challenges with confidence, and create a foundation for a more fulfilling and harmonious life.

Adaptability: Flexibility to adjust to new circumstances or unexpected changes. Adaptability helps you approach unfamiliar situations with an open mind and learn from the experience.

Self-Awareness: Understanding your strengths, weaknesses, emotions, and motivations. It's the foundation for personal growth, allowing you to identify areas for improvement and opportunities to grow.

Self-Discipline: The ability to control impulses and stay focused on long-term goals. Essential for avoiding distractions and staying on track toward your objectives.

Assertive Communication: Expressing your ideas and needs clearly and respectfully without being aggressive or passive. Builds healthy relationships and prevents unnecessary conflicts.

Active Listening: Paying full attention to what someone else is saying, showing interest and understanding. A crucial skill for effective communication and strengthening relationships.
~~~

Time Management: The ability to organize and plan your time efficiently to meet responsibilities and achieve goals. Enhances productivity and reduces stress.

Gratitude: Appreciating and valuing what you have, even during difficult times. Focusing on the positives improves emotional well-being.

Social Skills: Techniques for engaging with others effectively and positively. Includes empathy, active listening, and the ability to create meaningful connections.

Motivation: An internal drive that pushes you to act and achieve goals. Keeps you focused and helps overcome challenges along the way.

Negotiation: The ability to reach agreements that satisfy all parties involved. Involves finding common ground and being flexible to achieve mutually beneficial outcomes.

Proactivity: Taking initiative to act before problems arise, allowing you to control situations. Helps anticipate difficulties and find solutions before they become obstacles.

Conflict Resolution: Managing disagreements constructively. Requires effective communication, empathy, and the ability to find solutions that benefit everyone involved.

Problem-Solving: The ability to analyze situations and find effective solutions. A vital skill for tackling challenges and overcoming them practically.

Serenity: A state of calm and balance that allows you to act clearly and deliberately. Key for managing stress and making thoughtful decisions.

Decision-Making: The process of evaluating different options and choosing the best one. Involves analyzing potential consequences and acting confidently.

Teamwork: Collaborating with others to achieve a shared goal. Involves skills like communication, empathy, and cooperation to reach common objectives.

Tranquility: Inner peace that helps you handle situations with clarity. Fundamental for making sound decisions and staying composed under pressure.

~~~

PURPOSE AND FUTURE

This glossary explores the fundamental concepts related to finding purpose and building a meaningful future. Each term provides insights to help you discover your motivation, set clear goals, and navigate life with intention. By understanding these ideas, you can create a path that aligns with your values and aspirations, leading to a future filled with fulfillment and growth. As you apply these concepts, you'll find yourself more focused and resilient in the face of challenges, strengthening your ability to stay committed to your journey. This glossary serves as a guide to help you unlock your full potential and shape the life you desire.

Self-Confidence: Believing in your ability to achieve goals and create the future you desire. It's essential for making decisions and taking action with assurance.

Change: The process of transforming into a new reality. Embracing and adapting to change allows you to grow and face new challenges with resilience.
~~~

Personal Growth: A continuous journey of development and improvement to reach your full potential. It's vital for living a fulfilling and meaningful life.

Determination: An inner strength that drives you to keep moving forward despite obstacles. It's key to staying focused and achieving your goals.

Hope: A trust in the possibility of a better future and your ability to influence it. Hope provides the energy needed to tackle challenges and persevere.

Goals: Objectives that give direction and help you grow. Setting goals enables you to plan for the future and take actionable steps toward what you want to achieve.

Opportunity: A circumstance that offers the chance to improve and learn. Seizing opportunities is critical for personal growth and progress.

Optimism: A positive outlook rooted in the belief that you can achieve your goals. Optimism helps you approach challenges with an open and proactive mindset.

Planning: The process of organizing actions to achieve your goals. Planning provides a clear path toward the future you want to create.

Purpose: The reason or motivation that gives meaning to your actions. Having a purpose keeps you focused and helps you find significance even in challenging situations.

Renewal: The act of leaving the past behind and creating a new present. Renewal involves letting go of what no longer serves you and embracing new possibilities for improvement.

Overcoming: The act of facing and triumphing over difficulties, emerging stronger. It's vital for building a better future and learning from your experiences.

Transformation: A profound change that leads to a new way of being or seeing life. Transformation is the result of constant learning and growth from your experiences.

Vision: A clear picture of what you want to achieve in the future. Having a vision motivates and guides your decisions toward your objectives.

~~~

FREEDOM AND REDEMPTION

This glossary delves into the transformative concepts of freedom and redemption, offering a deeper understanding of their role in personal growth and healing. Each term is designed to inspire and empower you to break free from limitations, embrace change, and strive for a life of purpose and renewal. By exploring these ideas, you can embark on a journey toward liberation, forgiveness, and the realization of your true potential.

Repentance: Acknowledging a mistake and feeling a genuine desire to change. It is a fundamental step toward redemption and forgiveness.

Compassion: A feeling of empathy for yourself and others, coupled with the desire to ease suffering. Compassion is essential for forgiveness and emotional healing.

Dignity: The inherent value of every human being, which remains intact despite mistakes. Recognizing your intrinsic worth is vital for finding the path to redemption.
~~~

Hope: Belief in the possibility of a better future. Hope motivates you to keep pursuing your goals and seeking opportunities to improve.

Inner Strength: The ability to remain steadfast and resilient in the face of challenges. It helps you confront difficulties and move forward with determination.

Inner Freedom: The feeling of being free despite external circumstances, rooted in inner peace. It allows you to find serenity and strength regardless of what happens around you.

Emotional Liberation: The process of letting go of negative emotions such as resentment and guilt. Emotional liberation enables you to live more freely and focus on the present.

Forgiveness: Letting go of resentment and embracing the possibility of starting anew. Forgiveness is a liberating act that helps you release the past and move toward a fuller life.

Redemption: The act of freeing yourself from guilt or mistakes by striving to become better. Redemption involves acknowledging your faults and committing to change.

Renewal: A transformation that involves leaving behind old patterns and adopting new paths. Renewal is a vital part of personal growth and redemption.

Resilience: The capacity to adapt to and recover from difficult situations, emerging stronger. Resilience is key to overcoming challenges and moving forward.

Responsibility: The ability to accept the consequences of your decisions. Responsibility empowers you to learn from mistakes and take control of your future.

Healing: The process of emotional and mental recovery to achieve well-being. Healing helps you overcome pain and find balance.

Transformation: A profound change that leads you to become a better person. Transformation is the result of learning and the journey toward redemption.

~~~

BIBLIOGRAPHY

Cueva Pérez, S. Socioemotional Competencies in the Inmate Population [Undergraduate Thesis in Psychology]. Oviedo: University of Oviedo; 2024. Available at: https://digibuo.uniovi.es/dspace/handle/10651/73899.

Durán Zuazo, J.C. Personal Resilience Factors in Incarcerated Children Attending the Gran Bretaña School in the San Pedro Area of La Paz [Bachelor's Thesis in Psychology]. La Paz: Universidad Mayor de San Andrés; 2010. Available at: https://repositorio.umsa.bo/handle/123456789/35717.

Ferreira, A.I.A. de A. Social Reintegration of Former Inmates: A Case Study [Master's Dissertation, Iscte - Instituto Universitário de Lisboa]. Repositório Iscte; 2023. Available at: http://hdl.handle.net/10071/30388.

García-España, E., García-España, E. Social Reintegration of Inmates in Penitentiary Centers: A Criminological Analysis. Bol Criminol. 2024;(206):1-8. Available at: https://revistas.uma.es/index.php/boletin-criminologico/article/view/20600.

Gomes, M.S., Libório, L.A. Manna from Heaven: Religious Fantasy for the Elderly or Resilience in Life's Difficulties? Rev Int Apoyo Incl Logop Soc Multicult. 2020;6(1):98-108. Available at: https://revistaselectronicas.ujaen.es/index.php/riai/article/view/5214.

González Pérez, M. Resilience and Its Relationship with Social Adaptation in Inmates of a Penitentiary Center [Bachelor's Thesis in Psychology]. Mexico City: National Autonomous University of Mexico; 2019. Available at: http://repositorio.amapsi.org:8081/jspui/handle/123456789/32.

Herrera Medina, M.I. Resilience and Its Relationship with Aggressiveness in Juvenile Offenders [Bachelor's Thesis in Clinical Psychology]. Ambato: Technical University of Ambato; 2020. Available at: https://repositorio.uta.edu.ec/items/9cf22cd5-6587-4ffb-9fdc-3a3d0e847076.

Kleiberth Lenin Mora Aragón. The Participatory Orchestra: A Resilience and Social (Re)Integration Strategy in the Penitentiary Context [Doctoral Thesis in Arts]. Poitiers: University of Poitiers; 2024. Available at: https://theses.hal.science/tel-04767351/.

Macías-Garzón, G.X., Rodríguez-Leuro, Á.I. Teachers, Teachings, and Learnings in Penitentiary Educational Contexts: A Literature Review. I+D Rev Investig. 2023;18(2):89-103. Available at: http://sievi.udi.edu.co/ojs/index.php/ID/article/view/416.

Mansilla, M.A., Vergara, J.C. Intra- and Extra-Carceral Community Networks in Chile: Apaquism and Evangelical Volunteering. Rev Museo Antropol. 2023;16(2):245-258. Available at: https://dx.doi.org/10.31048/1852.4826.v16.n2.40134.

Mora Aragón, K.L. The Participatory Orchestra: A Resilience and Social (Re)Integration Strategy in the Penitentiary Context [Doctoral Thesis in Arts]. Poitiers: University of Poitiers; 2024. Available at: https://theses.hal.science/tel-04767351/.

Nóbrega, P.R.F. Life Values, Resilience, and Coping in Inmates and Non-Inmates [Master's Thesis in Psychology]. Covilhã: University of Beira Interior; 2015. Available at: https://ubibliorum.ubi.pt/handle/10400.6/5535.

Novais, F.A.G., Ferreira, J.A., Santos, E.R. dos. Transition and Adjustment of Inmates to the Prison Establishment. Psychologica. 2010;(52-II):209-241. Available at: https://impactum-journals.uc.pt/psychologica/article/view/1647-8606_52-2_9.

Sanhueza, G.E. Data and Prison Management: Tools for Reintegration? Rev Estud Polit Pub. 2023;9(2):85-96. Available at: https://dx.doi.org/10.5354/0719-6296.2023.71063.

Vargas Guzmán, W.C., García Alejo, M. Resilience, Psychosocial Understanding for Post-Prisoners of the National Penitentiary and Prison Institute in Colombia. Rev Cienc Soc. 2021;27(Extra 3):151-167. Available at: https://dialnet.unirioja.es/servlet/articulo?codigo=8081763.

Villanueva Conislla, M. Penitentiary Benefits and Accessibility to the Right to Work as a Guarantee of Social Reintegration Outside Prison 2021. Ciencia Latina. 2024;8(3):6539-57. Available at: https://www.ciencialatina.org/index.php/cienciala/article/view/11838.

Zevallos Vega, L.D. Analysis of Treatment Programs to Strengthen Positive Social Reintegration Outcomes in the Extra-Prison Population [Master's Thesis in Public Management]. Lima: Continental University; 2024. Available at: https://repositorio.continental.edu.pe/handle/20.500.12394/15363.

Zuluaga Gómez, A. Resilience: A Shield Against the Sordidness of Modern Times. Poiésis. 2013;4(7). Available at: https://revistas.ucatolicaluisamigo.edu.co/index.php/poiesis/article/view/578.

~~~

Don't miss out!

Visit the website below and you can sign up to receive emails whenever Arturo José Sánchez Hernández publishes a new book. There's no charge and no obligation.

https://books2read.com/r/B-A-RZZWB-LQBIF

BOOKS 2 READ

Connecting independent readers to independent writers.

Did you love *Rebirth Behind Bars*? Then you should read *Challenging Loneliness*[1] by Arturo José Sánchez Hernández!

[2]

"Challenging Loneliness: Paths to Reconnect" is a practical and comforting guide that addresses this state of isolation in the modern world. By integrating deep analysis, inspiring proverbs, and beautiful images, the book explores the causes of feeling disconnected and offers effective strategies to overcome this state. Readers will learn to strengthen existing bonds and form new ones, transforming loneliness into an opportunity for personal growth and deeper relationships. Ideal for those looking to revitalize their social and emotional interactions, this manual becomes an essential resource for reconnecting with oneself and others.

---

1. https://books2read.com/u/b5KXlk

2. https://books2read.com/u/b5KXlk

Also by Arturo José Sánchez Hernández

Adolescentes con Propósito

Propósito en Marcha

Detti illustrati

Virtù cardinali

Chiavi per sedurre con efficacia

Dictons illustrés

Vertus Cardinals

Clés Pour Séduire Efficacement

Attitudes Puissantes

Décide avec Sagesse

Ditados Ilustrados

Virtudes Cardinais

Chaves Para Conquistar Com Eficácia

Guérison et croissance personnelle

Quand l'amour s'achève

Healing and Personal Growth

When Love Ends

Challenging Loneliness

Rebirth Behind Bars

Illustrated sayings

Cardinal Virtues

Keys to Effective Seduction

Powerful Attitudes

Decide Wisely

Jugendliche mit Zweck

Zweck in Aktion

Sanación y Crecimiento Personal

Cuando el Amor Termina

Desafiando la Soledad

Renacer entre Rejas

Teens with Purpose

Purpose in Action

About the Author

Arturo José Sánchez Hernández, born in Havana in 1970, is a physician specializing in Comprehensive General Medicine and Psychiatry. He has an extensive professional and academic background, supported by several publications focused on ethics and the theory of values.

With notable experience in sexuality and couple and family psychotherapy, Dr. Sánchez Hernández has devoted part of his career to exploring these areas of mental health. Additionally, he is distinguished as an author of self-help and personal growth books, where sayings and images play a central role.

He currently resides in Maun, Botswana, where he practices as a psychiatrist at the Letsholathebe II Memorial Hospital. His commitment to mental health and individual well-being has made him a highly regarded professional both in his home country and in his new community in Botswana.

www.ingramcontent.com/pod-product-compliance
Lightning Source LLC
LaVergne TN
LVHW091105150826
845673LV00002B/721